Teaching
Phonics
for Balanced Reading

This book is dedicated to my two grandchildren, Griffin and Robyn,
who enjoy their grandpa's stories almost as much as their grandpa enjoys telling them.

Teaching
Phonics
for Balanced Reading

EDMUND V. STARRETT   **SECOND EDITION**

CORWIN PRESS
A SAGE Publications Company
Thousand Oaks, CA 91320

For information:

Corwin Press
A Sage Publications Company
2455 Teller Road
Thousand Oaks, California 91320
www.corwinpress.com

Sage Publications Ltd.
1 Oliver's Yard
55 City Road
London EC1Y 1SP
United Kingdom

Sage Publications India Pvt. Ltd.
B-42, Panchsheel Enclave
Post Box 4109
New Delhi 110 017 India

Printed in the United States of America.

Library of Congress Cataloging-in-Publication Data

Starrett, E. V.
Teaching phonics for balanced reading / Edmund V. Starrett. — 2nd ed.
    p. cm.
Includes bibliographical references and index.
ISBN 1-4129-3919-4 or 978-1-4129-3919-5 (cloth : alk. paper)
ISBN 1-4129-3920-8 or 978-1-4129-3920-1 (pbk. : alk. paper)
    1. Reading—Phonetic method. 2. English language—Phonetics.
3. Reading (Elementary) I. Title.
LB1573.3.S74 2007
372.46′5—dc22

                                                          2006014228

This book is printed on acid-free paper.

06 07 08 09 10   10 9 8 7 6 5 4 3 2 1

Acquisitions Editor:	Cathy Hernandez
Editorial Assistant:	Charline Wu
Production Editor:	Jenn Reese
Copy Editor:	Thomas Burchfield
Typesetter:	C&M Digitals (P) Ltd.
Proofreader:	Caryne Brown
Indexer:	Nara Wood
Cover Designer:	Rose Storey
Graphic Designer:	Lisa Riley

Contents

Preface

THE IMPORTANCE OF PHONICS

It is important to point out at the beginning that, even though this book concentrates primarily on providing instruction in phonemic awareness and phonics, this is not the only method of teaching reading. Phonics is simply a part—a very important part—of a total reading program that includes such factors as fluency, silent reading, vocabulary development, and, most important, comprehension. Efficient reading programs should also include elements of whole language and word identification. Without any one of these essential parts, building an effective reading program will be greatly hampered.

Recent research from the National Reading Panel (2000) has shown that phonemic awareness and phonics are a proven and effective method of learning how to read and that all students benefit from systematic and explicit phonics instruction. A long of line of extensive research, by Adams (1998) and others, has concluded that the two best predictors of early reading success are alphabet recognition and phonemic awareness.

The evidence is now overwhelming that phonics works well for most children. Yet many elementary teachers today find themselves ill prepared to teach phonemic awareness or phonics—but not through any fault of their own. For the last twenty years, in many colleges of education, phonics has been ignored or taught in a superficial way while ideas about whole language have been promoted as the latest method of teaching reading.

Most educators now realize the importance of phonemic awareness and phonics, especially in beginning reading programs, and are searching for materials and ideas on how to implement them in the classroom. There is no shortage of material when it comes to learning about one particular aspect of phonemic awareness or phonics, but rarely can one find a source that covers all the aspects of phonics so that the teacher gets to see it in its wider aspects and relationships. *Teaching Phonics for Balanced Reading* lays a good foundation for understanding phonics in all of its aspects and gives practical examples and illustrations of how it may be used in the classroom.

ABOUT THIS BOOK

While recognizing the value of other methods of teaching reading, and other aspects of reading—vocabulary development, comprehension, etc.— *Teaching Phonics for Balanced Reading* presents only material that emphasizes the phonological and structural analysis aspects of reading. The focus here is on providing teachers and educators with a solid grounding in phonics and guidance on teaching phonics as part of a balanced reading program.

The goal of this book is to explain the content and ideas of teaching phonics in such a way that they can be easily understood by those who have little information about how phonics might be used in the classroom, while also keeping the content technical enough for readers with more advanced understanding. *Teaching Phonics for Balanced Reading* is intended as a reference book, not as a textbook to be read once and then set aside. It is hoped that teachers will want to keep this book in their classrooms—to be used in making lesson plans or for informational purposes.

Each topic in *Teaching Phonics for Balanced Reading* is presented in such a way as to be general enough to cover the entire field yet specific enough to be of practical value. Principles of phonics are explicitly laid out. Rules and generalizations are enumerated and explained. In the section on blends and digraphs, for example, the reader will be exposed to all, or almost all, of the blends and digraphs. And when standards are discussed, specific examples will be given. All rules and examples are integrated into practical guidance on teaching phonics. The goal is for the reader to not only gain specific knowledge and examples of each topic but also see the day-to-day application of that knowledge in the classroom.

Chapter One opens the book with a historical perspective on the debate regarding the best way to teach reading, followed by a discussion of current research on phonemic awareness and phonics and how it can be used in the classroom.

Chapter Two tackles some of the concerns teachers have about teaching phonics, the problems involved in teaching letter-sound relationships, and the good news about phonics. This chapter should give teachers a better understanding of the order and sequencing of phonics instruction as well as insights into how it may be integrated in the classroom.

Chapter Three discusses the need to learn to identify, sound out, and reproduce the letters of the alphabet and the difficulties involved in this learning. At the end of the chapter, readers will find several activities that can be beneficial in augmenting the learning of the alphabet and its sounds. For many teachers, this is the most important chapter in the book, as so many reading problems have their origin at the very beginning stages of learning to read (for example, when first learning the alphabet).

Chapters Four through Six contain material about consonants, vowels, and syllabication. Each of these chapters starts with ideas and concepts that are easy to understand or less complex, and then proceeds to the more complicated ideas. The structure of each chapter represents the ascending order by which a teacher generally tries to introduce material to students. Rules and generalizations are presented in order to help teachers determine which ones are worth teaching or explaining to students and which ones have little or no value. It is generally conceded that rote memorization of most of these generalizations is a waste of time and serves little or no educational purpose. On the other hand, it is helpful for teachers to be aware of them as part of their knowledge and understanding of English orthography. Plenty of occasions will arise when this knowledge can be put to good use. Suggested classroom activities are interspersed throughout these chapters, placed near the discussion of relevant phonics topics.

Chapter Seven contains a discussion of educational standards for kindergarten through fifth grade as they relate to reading and phonics. In 2002 with the passage of No Child Left Behind and Reading First legislation, which were based on the findings of the National Reading Panel, educational reform efforts began to change how reading was being taught on the local, state, and national levels. This legislation opened up a whole new age of accountability for everyone involved in education—students, parents, teachers, administrators, local boards of education, and state departments of education—as they began working together toward the same objective: full literacy and mathematical proficiency for all students by 2014. Every state and school district set up grade level standards in reading to be achieved by all students. Two examples of these grade-level standards—the first from the state of Texas and the other created by the International Reading Association—can be found in Resource A: Standards for Elementary Education.

The last chapter, Chapter Eight, comprises informal tests, or assessments, that teachers can use to evaluate certain segments of phonemic awareness and word analysis skills. These assessments are specifically designed so that the teacher can quickly evaluate whether or not the child has mastered a particular skill. Using them for diagnostic or informal assessment purposes, the teacher can take note of each student's level of understanding and plan accordingly.

It must be pointed out that the manner in which the material is presented in each chapter does not necessarily reflect the exact order in which the material should be presented or learned in the classroom. As indicated earlier, the content of each chapter generally begins with the simpler concepts and proceeds from there to those that are more complicated or difficult to understand. The examples given for each lesson also proceed from simpler to more complex, and generally contain familiar sounds or words that students use in their active vocabulary. The particular order in which teachers may use these examples, however, will differ as the teachers' needs differ. Instead of trying to use everything in this book in the exact order presented here, it is hoped that readers will pick and choose whatever material or ideas they find helpful and use them as the need occurs.

In conclusion, it is worth emphasizing that there are no miracle cures when it comes to teaching reading. No one type of program or method by itself will automatically lead all children to be successful in reading. The most important factor for the success or failure of any program is the attitude of the teacher. When a teacher has knowledge of a particular method, sees the application of the method for her students, and believes the method will work, there's a good chance that even a poorly researched program will be successful. When a teacher lacks knowledge of, or does not believe in, a particular method, even the best-conceived program is destined for failure.

This book was written with the hope and expectation that teachers will gain additional knowledge of phonics, see its value and application for their classrooms, and come to believe in the techniques enough so that the information provided here will make them better teachers.

Acknowledgments

Special thanks to Fred Acerri, a reference services consultant for Wayne County [Michigan] Regional Educational Service Agency, for all the assistance he gave me regarding using the Internet for my research. To Richard Kunzi, principal of McDowell Elementary in Taylor, Michigan, for his warm friendship and continuous encouragement in my writing activities. To Jean Ward, Sue Schumer, Cathy Hernandez, and Charline Wu for their encouragement and professional guidance throughout this long writing process. A special thanks goes to Cathy Shapiro and Thomas Burchfield, who guided the final editing and helped make the book more coherent. To my wife, Monica, who made many sacrifices to help me achieve the important goal of writing this book.

PUBLISHER'S ACKNOWLEDGMENTS

Corwin Press gratefully acknowledges the contributions of the following reviewers:

Jane Ching Fung, First Grade Teacher
Alexander Science Center School, Los Angeles, CA

Karen Kersey, Second Grade Teacher
Alban Elementary School, St. Albans, WV

Patti Green, Kindergarten Teacher
Will Rogers Elementary School, Ardmore, OK

Jeanne Gren, First Grade Teacher
Woodburn Elementary School, Morgantown, WV

Jennifer Palmer, Reading Specialist
Forest Lakes Elementary School, Forest Hills, MD

Adrian Rodgers, Assistant Professor of Teaching and Learning
The Ohio State University, Newark, OH

Peggy Rogers, First Grade Teacher
Burton Elementary School, Rexburg, ID

About the Author

 **Edmund V. Starrett** is a retired elementary teacher who has taught remedial reading and has several years' experience as a districtwide reading coordinator. He has also been involved in programs for the mentally challenged and the gifted. He is the published author of several children's books, an educational game, and workbooks in reading and writing. Edmund received his Doctor of Education Degree from Wayne State University.

1

The Role of Phonics in Reading Instruction

Questions regarding the nature, extent, and role of phonics instruction in beginning reading programs are not a modern phenomenon. These concerns have existed in public education for over three hundred years. Throughout the history of reading instruction, phonics, like other methods, has had its high moments and its low moments—from being essential to being ignored. Today, thanks primarily to the findings of the National Reading Panel (NRP), phonemic awareness (which lays the foundation for phonics instruction) and phonics instruction itself are beginning to find their proper role in teaching reading.

HISTORY OF TEACHING READING

Although the content of reading instruction changed considerably in the first two centuries of public education in this country, there was very little change in the method of teaching reading. *What* was being taught— the Bible, morality, and patriotism—were much more important than *how* it was being taught. Beginning with *The New England Primer*, published in England in 1683, instruction in the alphabet and phonics was always

1

stressed first. The children first learned the letters, letter syllables, spellings of sounds, and then the reading text.

After *The New England Primer* came a long string of spelling books that were used to teach reading. The most famous of these was Noah Webster's *The American Spelling Book,* affectionately called "the blue-backed speller, which over a period of about thirty years became one of the best-selling readers of all time, with a total distribution of 24 million copies (Smith, 1986, p. 45). The first part of the speller contained rules and regulations, followed by lessons on learning the alphabet, syllable, and consonant combinations, and various word lists to be sounded out according to the number of syllables.

With the arrival of Horace Mann on the educational scene in the middle 1800s, however, the almost two hundred years of phonics-based reading programs came to a sudden end. Horace Mann, as secretary of the Massachusetts Board of Education, was so impressed by the order and universality of Prussian education, that he publicly denounced phonics and advocated the whole-word method of teaching reading. Mann (sometimes referred to as the "Father of Modern Education") was such a persuasive individual that his system gradually spread to other states. *The McGuffey Eclectic Reader* was published in 1857. This book stressed learning-appropriate sight words according to grade levels and an organized plan that controlled sentence length and vocabulary to match the developmental level of the child (Strickland, 1998). Comprehension became the key to reading, and phonics instruction was relegated to a limited role or neglected altogether. Over a period of seventy years, the whole-word method and controlled-vocabulary readers gradually became the dominant types of reading instruction (Smith, 2002).

In the 1920s, the noted educator William Gray pushed phonics into virtual oblivion by categorizing phonics as "heartless drudgery" and helped develop the famous *Dick and Jane* readers, which captured the attention of many educators (Gray & Arbuthnot, 1946). By the 1950s, these "basal readers," which followed the "whole-word, look-say, meaning-first, phonics-little-and-later approach" (Adams, 1998, p. 26), were used by almost all public school teachers.

Just as Horace Mann began to question the value of phonics a hundred years before, so too, reading authorities in the mid-1950s began to question the value of the whole-word philosophy of reading. First came the publication of Rudolph Flesch's *Why Johnny Can't Read* in 1955 and his stinging attack on the look-say method, which he believed to be the great destroyer of democracy and the American Dream. Although rejected by most educators for its lack of research, it nonetheless became a bestseller and was quoted widely by just about anyone who found fault with educational practices of that time. With the popular backlash at reading methods triggered by Flesch's book, many researchers tried to determine the best way to teach reading.

The most decisive answer to this issue came as a result of extensive research by Jeanne Chall and her subsequent 1967 book *Learning to Read:*

The Great Debate. Chall's three-plus years of research concluded that programs that emphasized systematic instruction in teaching letter-sound relationships (phonics) lead to higher achievement. Many subsequent studies, such as "The Cooperative Research Program in First Grade Reading Instruction," undertaken by Bond and Dykstra in 1997, tended to substantiate Chall's conclusions. With the publication of *Becoming a Nation of Readers: The Report of the Commission of Reading* (Anderson, Hillbert, Scott, & Wilkerson, 1985), the popularization of commercial programs such as *The Phonics Game* and *Hooked on Phonics,* and Marilyn Adams's 1990 classic *Beginning to Read: Thinking and Learning About Print,* which supported Chall's original findings, educators began to rethink the role and value of phonics instruction in the classroom.

As the pendulum of change once swung from phonics to look-say to whole language, by the close of the twentieth century the pendulum began to swing back to phonics.

Fortunately, as the twentieth century came to a close, the debate about the best way to teach reading and the rhetoric coming from all sides of the issue were beginning to subside. Over time most educators began to realize that this was not an either/or type of issue, but one that lent itself to common sense. The International Reading Association's position paper (1998) on the role of phonics in reading instruction sums it up this way: "Rather than engage in debates about whether phonics should or should not be taught, effective teachers of reading and writing ask when, how, how much, and under what circumstances phonics should be taught." Another educator put the issue in proper perspective when she cautioned teachers, "Don't spend time debating whether to teach phonics, spelling, grammar, and other skills of literacy. Do spend time discussing how to teach them in a way that contributes to the learner's self-improvement" (Strickland, 1995, p. 299).

At the beginning of the twenty-first century, two federal initiatives began to dramatically change the methods and emphasis of future reading programs. These were the initiation of a National Reading Panel (NRP) during the presidency of William Clinton, and No Child Left Behind (NCLB), initiated by President George W. Bush, which began to implement the previous recommendations of the NRP. These two initiatives reinstated the importance of phonemic awareness and phonics in beginning reading programs.

THE NATIONAL READING PANEL

Displeased by the high rate of illiteracy among young adults and the lack of reading progress in many school districts, especially among lower-economic groups, Congress, in 1997, decided to get involved. It asked the director of the National Institute of Child Health and Human Development (NICHD) along with the U.S. secretary of education to set up a national panel of experts to study what could be done about improving reading instruction. A panel of fourteen, composed of leading educators in reading research, representatives of colleges of education, and parents, was selected for this all-important task.

The initial responsibility, which took over two years to complete, was threefold. First, it set out to examine a variety of databases to determine what research had been conducted on how children learn to read. The panel selected research from over one hundred thousand reading research studies published since 1966 and another fifteen thousand that were published before that time and considered only those from that selection that met rigorous scrutiny for reliability and accuracy. Second, the National Reading Panel sought information from the public regarding their ideas about teaching reading and their understanding of research in this area. Regional public meetings were set up in several locations in the U.S. so that parents and others could express their concerns and ideas. Third, the NRP consulted with leading educators and organizations that had interest in the debate over reading instruction. The panel received input from 125 individuals and organizations, including classroom teachers, administrators, university faculty, researchers, and others (NRP, *Frequently Asked Questions*, 2005).

After two years, the panel completed its report and submitted a document entitled "The Report of the National Reading Panel: Teaching Children to Read" at a hearing before the U.S. Senate Appropriations Committee on Labor, Health and Human Services, and Education. This report provided analysis and discussion in five areas in reading: phonemic awareness, phonics, fluency, vocabulary, and text comprehension.

The report is a consensus doctrine based on the best judgments of diverse groups of researchers, individuals, and organizations whose sole purpose is to improve reading instruction in the U.S. A thirty-five-page summary report called "Report of the National Reading Panel: Teaching Children to Read" is available on the Internet and is highly recommended for anyone interested in the issues surrounding reading instruction.

Duane Alexander, the director of the NICHD, sums up the conclusions of the NRP as follows: "For the first time, we now have guidance based on evidence from sound scientific research on how best to teach children to read. The panel's rigorous scientific review identifies the most effective strategies for teaching reading" (NICHD, 2005, p.1).

THE FINDINGS OF THE NATIONAL READING PANEL

While recognizing the extreme importance of the last three areas of analysis and discussion in the NRP report discussed above—fluency, vocabulary, and comprehension—for the purposes of this book, we will restrict our discussion in the following section to the first two areas: phonemic awareness and phonics.

Phonemic awareness (PA): The report from the National Reading Panel showed that teaching children to manipulate phonemes in words was highly effective under a variety of teaching conditions with a variety of different learners across a wide range of grade and age levels. It stressed that teaching phonemic awareness to children significantly improves their reading more than instruction that lacked attention to phonemic awareness (NRP Findings, 2000).

Some of the findings of the National Reading Panel may be summarized as follows:

- Phonemic awareness can be taught and learned.
- Phonemic awareness instruction helps children learn to read.
- Phonemic awareness instruction helps children learn to spell.
- Phonemic awareness instruction is most effective when children are taught to manipulate phonemes by using letters of the alphabet.
- Phonemic awareness instruction is most effective when it is focused on only one or two types of phoneme manipulation, rather than on several types.

These findings substantiated earlier ones that concluded that phonemic awareness and phonics instruction were the two best indicators of success in reading (Adams, 1990).

Phonics: Concerning the value of teaching phonics, the NRP came to the following conclusions:

- Systematic (planned) phonics instruction produces significant benefits for all students in kindergarten through sixth grade, especially for children having a difficult time learning to read. First graders who were taught phonics were better able to decode and spell, and had better ability to comprehend printed material. Older students who were taught systematic phonics were better able to decode and spell, but their comprehension was not greatly improved.
- Systematic phonics benefits students with learning disabilities and low-achieving students who are not disabled.
- Systematic phonics instruction was significantly more effective in improving low economic status, children's alphabetic knowledge, and word-reading skills than instructional methods that were less focused on phonemic awareness.
- The early reading success of children in the kindergarten and first grades indicate that phonics instruction should be implemented at these grades and age levels.

The NRP report concluded that the facts and findings provide convincing evidence that explicit, systematic phonics instruction is a valuable and essential part of a successful classroom reading program

Teaching students the sound structure of language reduces the level of reading failure. Teaching students to blend sounds to create words and then to segment words into their individual component sounds are important features of a good reading program. "Simply immersing students in interesting stories or providing the occasional and unsystematic clue from time to time does not constitute effective teaching for students" (Hempenstall, 2003).

IMPORTANT CONSIDERATIONS FOR TEACHING PHONICS

In order to get a clearer understanding of just what is involved in the teaching of phonemic awareness and phonics, we first consider what it is not.

Phonics instruction is not a complete reading program by itself: Phonics is simply one part of the total program. Although it is a very important part of beginning reading programs, it cannot, by itself, guarantee reading success for all students. The benefits of phonics instruction will depend on the comprehensiveness and effectiveness of the entire literacy curriculum. Nor is phonics the only way to teach reading. Millions of students have learned to read with little or no exposure to any phonics.

We must keep in mind that the ultimate objective of teaching reading is not to teach children how to sound out (or "attack") words, but rather to help them to understand what is being read—i.e., comprehension. It should be pointed out that developing students' reading fluency and vocabulary and incorporating practices such as reading aloud, silent reading, and exposure to good literature, were all shown to have a positive effect on reading comprehension and should be implemented in addition to phonics instruction. Research shows that a combination of methods, rather than a single teaching method, leads to the best learning (NRP Report, 2000).

Phonics is not a one-size-fits-all program: Although phonics needs to be taught in a systematic, effective manner and is useful for class or group work, we must not conclude that phonics must always be taught in this manner, or that it is of equal value to everyone.

In the beginning, it is extremely helpful to have both whole class and small group participation, as both methods will benefit all students—especially those with lesser skills who often learn from the responses of their classmates. But as children progress in developing skills, some of them will need more help than others and will be working at different levels. Some students will be engaged in easier types of instruction (e.g., identifying initial sounds in words), while other may be engaged in more advanced types (segmentation of words, deletions, etc.). As time goes on, group participation becomes less important while individual instruction becomes more important.

The best way to proceed is to assess individual needs before instruction. That way the teacher has some idea of the particular needs of each student and then can plan instruction along those lines. Hopefully, by the end of the second grade or thereabouts, there will less and less need for phonics for most students.

Phonics instruction should not be about rules and drills: As had often occurred in the past, phonics programs required that students memorize rules, even when the rules were not consistent, and spent sixty percent or more of their time on workbook activities and little time actually reading. Studies indicate that although a particular rule or generalization may be useful for application for a group of words being studied, students need not necessarily memorize the rule (Clymer, 1963). Today in most schools, students spend less time on workbook activities. Today we teach students only those phonics generalizations that are most prevalent in our language (Block & Israel, 2005).

Phonemic awareness and phonics instruction should not be boring: Teaching phonics should be "phun." Yopp (1992) gave five general recommendations for phonemic awareness activities:

- Keep a sense of playfulness and fun; avoid drill and rote memorization.
- Use group settings that encourage interaction among children.
- Encourage children's curiosity about language and their experience with it.
- Allow for, and be prepared for, individual differences.
- Make sure the tone of the activity is not evaluative but rather fun and informal.

Unlike other academic subjects, explicit phonics instruction should not consume much classroom time, even in kindergarten. For best results, the sessions should be short—fifteen to twenty minutes—and restricted to one or two concepts. They should be varied in nature and involve student participation and interaction. In a normal school year, approximately twenty hours of phonemic awareness and/or phonics instruction would be sufficient (National Institute for Literacy, 2005).

For most students, the time spent on phonics instruction should be less and less for the first three years. If some children are still in need of additional instruction, it should be provided in daily tutorial sessions, pullout programs, or afterschool activities.

Phonics instruction lends itself nicely to inclusion in spelling and writing classes since all three are interrelated. Reading is decoding, i.e., making sounds from letters. Spelling is encoding—that is, making letters from sounds. Writing is the decoding of sounds into written letters. Each subject area reinforces the other. Presenting phonics in the context of spelling and writing not only reinforces the skills, but also lends a greater variety to the activity. In other words, phonics is not just about reading—it's about spelling and writing as well.

PHONICS FOR ENGLISH LANGUAGE LEARNERS

The results from the National Reading Panel have clearly demonstrated that phonemic awareness activities and explicit phonics instruction are more relevant for minority and low socioeconomic-status children. But do these methods work for the increasing number of students who are entering our schools with little background in English? The answer is a resounding yes—phonics instruction is effective for English language learners.

When working with students who are learning English while learning to read, teachers must use instructional materials that are of interest to students. In addition, these students need to use materials that will enable them to experience reading success (Jesness, 2005, pp. 8–11). All instruction should be positive and relevant, but in the case of English language learners, even more so.

Strategies for Teaching Reading to English Language Learners

As a preparation for learning to read, English teachers should encourage parents to read to their children at home in their primary language. Research and theory both show that there is a carryover from reading in the primary language and learning to read English. As English literacy grows, the primary language skills begin to transfer to reading in English (Peregoy & Boyle, 1997).

Getting Started: As soon as possible, teachers should get their students started on a reading program that not only emphasizes phonemic awareness and phonics skills, but also is presented to them at their interest level. Too many easy-to-read books that are written with younger children in mind are a turnoff to older readers. The trick is to find material that presents basic skills on the students' interest level.

Use phonics readers: Fortunately, there are a growing number of publishers who have chapter books that promote development of phonological skills. For younger readers, for example, there are *Dr. Maggie's Classroom Phonics Readers*, a set of twenty-four books that develop progressive skills with attractive formats and follow-up. For older readers, there is *READ XL*, published by Scholastic Press, designed to fit the needs of special education and older, struggling readers. Both these series align with the objectives of No Child Left Behind for phonics, fluency, vocabulary, and comprehension. There is also federal money available under NCLB that can be used to purchase these materials.

Teach high-frequency words as whole words: At the same time that the children are beginning some independent reading in material that stresses phonemic awareness, it is recommended that they also begin learning high-frequency words as whole (or sight) words. There are two reasons for this. The first is that many high-frequency words are not phonetic (e.g., *was, come, is, one, two, laugh*) and therefore need to be taught as sight words. Second, the high-frequency words (e.g., *ball, sing,* and *day*) that are phonetic can be learned first as sight words. As language skills develop, phonetic words can be used later to sound out new or unfamiliar words. Research tells us that having a large sight vocabulary is invaluable in helping to identify words (Heilman, Blair & Rupley, 1998, p. 152).

There are several prepackaged, high-frequency word lists (i.e., flash cards) that can be purchased at the local teacher's store. These lists, and many others, are also available free of charge on the Internet. Two of the better-known word lists are those compiled by Edward Fry, and the old standby (and still reliable) Dolch Basic Sight Word List.

Teaching Phonograms: If teachers are uncertain just where to begin instruction for older students who are just beginning to learn to read English, a good place to start would be with the phonograms. These word families are short and phonetically consistent, and generally represent common high-frequency words that are often used in print. Learning one phonogram easily leads to learning many other words of similar sound and nature. Learning phonograms also assists in the sounding-out process that is so necessary for figuring out (by sounding out) unfamiliar words. For the many common words that are irregularly spelled or are not phonetic, flash cards could be provided so that the words are learned as sight words.

Another approach is to start with rime phonograms; (The word *rime* is used here to distinguish it from the more traditional term *rhyme* as used in relation to poetry) knowing that *strain* and *drain* rime, may allow learning *main* and *brain* by analogy (Hempenstall, 2003). It has been demonstrated with dyslexic students that the learning of onsets and rimes is one of the most effective ways of promoting phonemic awareness activities that are so essential for beginning reading and spelling (Bowen & Francis, 1991).

It is important to keep all instructions short and to the point and to keep an accurate accounting both of skills learned and those to be learned. A phonetic skills checklist such as the one presented in Resource C would be helpful for tracking purposes.

Using Web Sites: I would be remiss, at this point, if I didn't mention what a marvelous resource the World Wide Web is, especially in providing high-interest texts for readers. More and more Web sites on the Internet now contain material, stories, and essays written by children of all grade levels that can be viewed and reproduced free of charge.

THE NEED FOR A BALANCED READING PROGRAM

While phonics instruction is important, other methods that put emphasis on learning whole words also have a role, especially at the beginning stages of reading, to get children started. There are dozens of very common and high-frequency words (e.g., *one, laugh, love, come, does, two, gone*) that defy phonetic analysis and may be better taught as whole words.

Whole language and other linguistic approaches, which attempt to apply scientific knowledge of language to reading, have a valuable coordinating role of putting the reading process in a broader perspective and directing it toward the ultimate end of reading—comprehension. It is difficult to conceive of anyone becoming a good teacher of reading by using only one method exclusively. As several authorities put it, "Any strategy of reading instruction based on a single principle is incomplete, no matter how valid the principle" (Smith, Goodman, & Meredith, 1970, p. 270). This concept was reinforced in a national survey of elementary teachers' beliefs and priorities regarding the best methods of teaching reading. It concluded that the majority of teachers embraced a balanced, eclectic approach to elementary reading instruction, blending phonics and holistic principles and practices (Bauman, Hoffman, Moon, & Duffy-Hester, 1998).

Teachers need to be more like doctors in their approach to their profession. Doctors find out what's wrong with their patients before they prescribe the medicine. Some teachers prescribe the medicine before they know what's wrong with the students. Doctors may prescribe an aspirin for some patients and minor surgery for others, and a few may need a heart transplant. Doctors would be very limited in what they could do for their patients if they were restricted to one size of bandage to cover every sore, one type of needle for every injection, or the same prescription for every ailment. So teachers need to be specialists too. Some children may just need a little shot of encouragement to get going; others, at times, may need a specific medicine for a specific need. Hopefully, only a few will need life-saving help. No two children are exactly alike. No two needs are exactly the same. No one approach will solve all their problems. Everything else being equal, the more teachers know about phonetic principles, psycholinguistics, miscue analysis, whole-language concepts, and other theories of learning—with all their strengths and weaknesses—the more likely they are to have the right kind of medicine at the right time to cure the needs of all their students.

In all of this, it must be remembered that methods of teaching reading, by themselves, solve nothing. It's how and when the methods are used and applied that makes the difference between success and failure. Teaching reading is more than just a science; it's an art.

THE "TEACHER EFFECT"

More than anything else, teachers of reading ought to be aware of an underlying principle that directly affects the total outcome of efforts. This principle, which is so hard to detect or even define, is called "teacher effect." Simply put, it means that if teachers don't understand or believe in what they are expected to do, they will sabotage even the best of programs and make them ineffective (Stahl, Duffy-Hester, & Dougherty Stahl, 1998). This can happen even when the teachers think they are following the lesson plans or prescribed curriculum. *The two key ingredients of making any educational program work effectively, then, are knowledge of the subject and belief in the system.*

"Teacher effect" partially explains why teachers in the same grade level, using the same system and materials, can produce dramatically different results and, inversely, why teachers using different systems and materials can produce the same results as others using different systems. When it comes to teaching phonemic awareness, phonological awareness, and structural analysis of words, the conclusion is obvious: The teacher needs training in this field and must believe that the system will work. As one authority put it:

> The "teacher effect" [research] tells us that teachers need to be given a clear rationale for being asked to change their methods for teaching reading. The new method has to make sense and be designed so that it works in the classroom, with curriculum materials and lesson plans. The teacher must be thoroughly trained, so that she feels confident and comfortable with the new approach. (McGuinness, 1997, pp. 171–172)

CONCLUSION

After many years of trying to determine the role of phonics in reading programs, it is probably safe to say that we may now have some good answers. It seems from an abundance of research, not only from the National Reading Panel and the International Reading Association, but from other sources as well, that the best way to teach reading is through a systematic, explicit presentation of phonemic awareness activities and phonics skills. Finally, almost all educators and authorities agree that the two best predictors of early reading success are alphabetic recognition and phonemic awareness.

The re-emphasis on phonics, however, does not mean a return to the "bad old days" of "drill and kill" but has ushered in with it a refreshing enthusiasm for new and innovative ways to teach phonetic concepts.

Never in the history of education in the United States have early elementary teachers been more creative and resourceful in helping children learn to read. More and more teachers are reading, and rereading, favorite nursery rhymes, poems, and stories to their students. Children in kindergarten are learning the alphabet through song, dance, and making their own alphabet books. They are learning phonemes and syllabication through clapping or chanting. They are learning sound relationships through alliteration, tongue twisters, onsets, and rimes. They are learning to read independently and with a partner. They are involved in making their own signs and writing letters and words. They now have TV, videos, CDs, games, and computers to assist whenever they may be needed. The hundreds of ways to make these activities enjoyable and effective are limited only by the teacher's imagination.

Reading programs today have become so full of variety that kindergarten and first grade students must look forward to reading and reading instruction more than ever. Who can get bored? Who cannot learn in a situation full of excitement and variety as exists in today's classroom?

2

Understanding Phonics

One of the reasons disagreement on phonics still exists in some quarters is that not everyone—not even the experts themselves—understands just what is meant by "teaching phonics." The definition of phonics, the extent of phonics instruction, the sequencing of instruction, even the time and place of instruction, have all been the subjects of heated debate for the last half century.

COMMON RESERVATIONS ABOUT TEACHING PHONICS

Confusing Terminology: Ask two teachers to define phonics, and you'll probably get two different answers. The terms *phonetics, phonics,* and *phonemic awareness* are sometimes used interchangeably, although each term has a different emphasis and a different meaning.

Phonetics can be defined as "that segment of linguistic science, which deals with speech sounds, how these sounds are made vocally, sound changes which develop in language, and the relation of speech sounds to the total language process" (Heilman, 1966, p. 2).

Phonics, on the other hand, "refers to a system of teaching reading that builds on the alphabetic principle, a system of which a central component is the teaching of correspondence between letters or groups of letters and their pronunciation" (Adams, 1998, p. 50).

Phonemic awareness is "the understanding, or insight, that a word is made up of a series of discrete sounds. . . . This awareness includes the ability to pick out and manipulate sounds in spoken words" (Blevins, 1998, p. 28). Phonemic awareness is generally considered the first step in phonics instruction and lays the foundation for more extensive phonics (Stahl, Duffy-Hester & Dougherty Stahl, 1998).

In other words, phonetics is the science of speech sounds; phonics is the application of that science in developing reading and spelling skills; and phonemic awareness has to do with individual sounds in words.

Just reading the three definitions above and trying to figure out how they may have relevance for a reading program, however, still leaves the teacher in limbo. The terms *phonics* and *phonemic awareness* are too narrow to explain the complexities involved in the reading process; and *phonetics* is too broad and complicated to have meaning for children who are learning how to read.

Confusing Methods: Another reason for the reluctance of some to use phonics instruction in the classroom lies in the fact that the reading program most teachers are currently using already contains some phonics. If teaching the "phonetic method" means simply teaching letter-sound relationships, almost all methods of teaching reading could be described as phonetic.

Another reason for the confusion lies in the fact that programs claiming to be phonics-based differ greatly from each other in many respects. In *Approaches to Beginning Reading*, R. C. Aukerman (1984) identified over 100 different phonics-type reading programs. Yet these same programs can be as different from each other as night and day. As one observer pointed out, "They [phonics programs] differ in starting point as well as ending point, some beginning prior to what might be called phonics proper and most extending beyond. They differ in methods, materials, procedures, and everything taught in between.... They differ in fundamental strictures and assumptions about what to and what not to teach, about how to and how not to teach" (Adams, 1998, p. 52). These differences are not in teaching style or procedure alone, but often also involve genuine conflicts and incompatibilities.

Since phonics programs involve so many different approaches, techniques, and philosophies, and since no one program can be pointed out as a model of what a good phonics program ought to be, it is not difficult to understand why there is such confusion and controversy about the subject.

Unanswered Questions: Because of the confusion mentioned above and the polarizing rhetoric still coming from some educators, teachers have many questions about teaching phonics. Should we teach words in isolation? What about drills? What kinds of drills are we talking about? How long and how many? Should phonics instruction take place only in context (i.e., implicit), or can it be isolated (i.e., explicit)? How do word analysis skills fit into the picture? What method works best for all my students?

Still others are reluctant to teach phonics because of past experiences with it. They have an uncomfortable feeling that phonics is not only too old-fashioned for our modern world, but that it also conjures up thoughts of making reading class a series of drills ("drill and kill"), repetitions ad nauseam, and rote memorization of rules that are inconsistent at best. They are afraid reading class will go backward to the days "when kids never saw anything that wasn't purple—the color of old-fashioned ditto sheets" (Jones, 1996, p. 4).

These teachers might equate phonics with boring and unrealistic sentences, such as "The cat sat on a hat," or "Let men set a net," where the learning of a particular sound becomes more important than understanding what is read. For a few teachers, their memory of, and experience with, phonics carries a lot of baggage and brings back haunting recollections of what they themselves went through while learning to read. As in other facets of life, it is often the abuses of the system, or the extremes of the positions, that one remembers most to the detriment of the whole.

With a clearer understanding of phonics and English orthography, these reservations can be banished. This chapter should help teachers begin to see through the fog that seems to surround phonics. The purpose of this book is to help teachers become well informed and confident of their knowledge about phonics so that they can use it as part of an effective reading program.

WHAT IS PHONEMIC AWARENESS?

Like many other facets of phonics, there is a great deal of confusion or misunderstanding about the terminology used to describe phonemic awareness. Phonemic awareness (PA) is a relatively new term for an old concept; twenty or thirty years ago, one hardly heard the term at all. Phonemic awareness was then simply called auditory discrimination, or beginning phonics.

Today there are many different synonyms for phonemic awareness, some of which are used incorrectly, and other synonyms that are used to denote a much broader concept. Depending on the author and/or the background of the reader, it has often been mistaken for other similar terms: auditory discrimination, phonological awareness, auditory analysis, sound categorization, phonetic segmentation, phonological sensitivity, and phonemic analysis, among others (Hempenstall, 2003).

Since this is such an important aspect for beginning instruction in reading, it is important to have a clear understanding of what phonemic awareness is all about. Anderson briefly defined phonemic awareness as "the understanding that words are composed of a sequence of individual sounds" (Anderson, 2003, p. 38). The National Right to Read Foundation extends the definition a little more: "Phonemic awareness is an understanding that words are made up of sounds and being able to hear, recognize, and manipulate the individual sounds that make up a word. For example, it is the ability to recognize (that) the word 'mom' is made up of separate sounds /m/ /o/ /m/" (Gagen, 2005). In other words, phonemic awareness is literally "sound" awareness.

Phonemic awareness: as the name implies, deals exclusively with phonemes, the smallest unit of sounds in the spoken language. Phonemes are different from letters, which often combine together as blends to make one sound. There are twenty-six letters in the English language, yet there are approximately forty-five phonemes. The word *go* has two letters and two distinct sounds: /g/o/. The word *show* has four letters and just two phonemes: /sh/o/.

Phonemic awareness should also not be confused with syllables, which are also sounds within words. A syllable is a word part that contains a vowel sound; a phoneme is the sound (or sounds) within a syllable. The word *understanding*, for example, has four syllables—un-der-stand-ing—while the number of phonemes more than doubles—/u/n/d/er/st/a/n/d/i/ng/.

Phonemic awareness is often confused with phonics instruction, which entails using letter-sound relationships to teach children to read and spell. Phonemic awareness is the initial stage of phonics when it involves teaching children to hear sounds in words in segmenting sounds, and to manipulate sounds within words. Phonemic awareness lays the foundation for later instruction in reading and writing. Without the ability to hear and distinguish sounds within words, all later types of phonics instruction are greatly delayed and/or become of little value. "The reason is obvious: children who cannot hear and work with the phonemes of the spoken language will have a difficult time learning how to relate these phonemes to the graphemes when they see them in printed words" (Ambruster, Lehr, & Osborn, 2005, p. 4).

The report from the National Reading Panel describes six activities that fall under the heading of phonemic awareness:

- *Phoneme isolation:* recognizing individual sounds in words. ("What is the first sound you hear in *hen*?" "What is the last sound you hear in *fat*?")
- *Phoneme identity:* recognizing the same sound in different words. ("What sound to you hear in *Bill, been, but*?" "What sound do you hear in *sun, set, sip*?")
- *Phoneme categorization:* recognizing the word with a different sound in a sequence of three or four words. ("Which word sounds differently: *sit, mit, fat . . . bus, bun, rug*?")
- *Phoneme blending:* listening to a sequence of separately spoken sounds and combining them to form a recognizable word. ("What word is /s/k/u/1?" Answer: *school*. "What word is /b/a/t/?" Answer: *bat*.)
- *Phoneme segmentation:* breaking a word into sounds by tapping out or counting the sounds or by pronouncing or positioning a marker for each sound. ("Tap out the number of phonemes you hear in *when*." Answer: three: /wh/e/n.)
- *Phoneme deletion:* recognizing what word remains when a specified phoneme is removed. ("What is *smile* without the /s/?" Answer: *mile*.)

Phonics: The second term that needs clarification and a brief explanation is the term *phonics.* Phonics instruction teaches children the relationship between the letters (graphemes) of the written language and the individual sounds (phonemes) of the spoken language. It teaches children to use these relationships to read and write words (NIFL, 2005).

Knowing these letter-to-sound relationships enables the reader to recognize familiar words and to "sound out," or decode, new or unfamiliar words. In short, phonics instruction is an application of the alphabetic principle—the understanding that there are systematic and predictable relationships between written letters and spoken language.

The key to phonics instruction is that it should be explicit and systematic and well planned.

Systematic Phonics: refers to an organized program in which letter-sound clusters are directly taught, blended, practiced in words and word families, and practiced initially in text with a high percentage of decodable words linked to phonics lessons (*California Initiative in Reading*, 1996). This means that phonics instruction should be well planned and taught in a prescribed sequence. The reading material supplied to the students should reinforce the particular phonics skill being taught. Many phonics programs use decodable books or texts in which all or most of the words are easy to decode by applying the phonics skills the child is learning. Additional blocks of time and opportunities must be set aside for reading and writing activities so that children can practice and reinforce what they have learned in phonics.

Explicit Phonics: refers to lessons or programs that provide precise directions for the teaching of these relationships.

The U.S. government's publication *Putting Children First* (2005) lists six approaches, or methods, for teaching phonemics. The distinction between programs is not absolute, and some programs of instruction combine several of these methods.

1. *Synthetic Phonics:* Children learn how to convert letters or letter combinations into sounds and then how to blend the sounds together to form recognizable words.

2. *Analytic Phonics:* Children learn to analyze letter-sound relationships in previously learned words. They do not pronounce words in isolation.

3. *Analogy-based Phonics:* Children learn to use parts of word families that they know to help identify words that they don't know that have similar parts.

4. *Phonics Through Spelling:* Children learn to segment words into phonemes and to make words by writing letters for phonemes.

5. *Embedded Phonics:* Children are taught letter-sound relationships during the reading of connected text.

6. *Onset-rhyme Phonics Instruction:* Children learn to identify the sound of the letter, or letters, before the first vowel (the onset) in a one-syllable word and the sounds of the remaining part of the word (the rhyme).

HOW PHONICS IS DEFINED IN THIS BOOK

So far, we have had an overview of the confusion regarding the exact definition of phonics and what constitutes a phonetic reading program. Now, for the sake of clarity, let us go into more detail about the definition of the term *phonics* as it is used here. In this book, *phonics* will be interpreted in its broadest connotations.

Phonics includes the notion of phonemic awareness, or the understanding that speech is composed of a series of individual sounds or phonemes and the ability to discern individual sounds in spoken words.

Our definition of phonics includes an understanding of the alphabetical principle, or the realization that letters in words may stand for specific sounds. As the awareness of the alphabetical principle develops and increases, students begin to use that knowledge and apply it to more complex orthographies such as consonant blends, digraphs, diphthongs, and phonograms (Stahl et al., 1998).

Structural analysis also comes under the umbrella of phonics as it is defined in this book. Structural analysis is a method of learning words and their meanings by noting structural changes that differentiate between words having common roots (Heilman, 1966). These changes include the addition of inflectional endings, modification resulting in prefixes and suffixes being added to known words, and the combining of words to make compounds and contractions. The ability to sound out parts of words individually will help students determine the pronunciation and meaning of new words (Heilman, 1966).

Finally, phonics as defined here includes the concept of syllabication, or the ability to divide longer and unknown words into syllables in order to sound them out and arrive at meaning. This is a skill that is carried on and used in later life when literate adults encounter unknown names, words from other languages, or unfamiliar terminology.

THE REAL CHALLENGE OF TEACHING PHONICS

The major problem with trying to teach sound-letter relationships (and one of the main reasons teachers learn and use other approaches to teaching reading) stems directly from the fact that English is not a phonemic language. Unlike most other orthographies, or spelling systems, English does not have a perfect, or, in many cases, even a close or consistent relationship between letter and sound. Unlike other languages that have a more consistent relationship between sound and symbol, English has few completely consistent rules to assist in the pronunciation of words. Italian and Turkish use twenty-seven letters to represent twenty-seven basic sounds. German uses thirty-eight symbols for thirty-six sounds. The *Webster's New World Dictionary* (1998) shows that the forty-plus phonemes, or sounds, of English can be represented by 251 different spellings.

In English, a reader who tries to sound out unfamiliar words can just as easily be misled as helped by a letter or combination of letters. Picture the young reader who finds out, much to his embarrassment, that a single letter sound that he learned and applied to decode unfamiliar words in one situation may misdirect him in another situation. He learns that *no* and *go* have the long /o/ sound at the end of the word; then he applies the same reasoning to *do* and *to* and finds out he is wrong. He learns that the short /e/ sound is usually represented with a single *e*, then quickly runs across the many exceptions in words, such as *bread, said, many, friend, says, head,* etc. He learns how to pronounce the word *through*, then finds out that the combination *ough* can also be pronounced in seven other ways, as in *thought, though, tough, bough, bought, hiccough,* and *cough*.

Unlike most other languages of the world, one cannot be absolutely sure how to spell or write a word in English if one has only heard it spoken and never seen it written. Inversely, one cannot be absolutely sure how to pronounce a word if one only saw it in its written form but never heard it pronounced before. The problem of the inconsistent letter-sound relationship in English is humorously illustrated in the following limerick by an unknown author published by the Spelling Reform Association:

It Made the Children Schrique

A teacher whose spelling is unique
Thus wrote down the days of the weque.
The first is spelt, "Sonday"
The second day, "Munday"
And now a new teacher they seque.

(*Rhymes Without Reason*, n.d.)

CORRELATING PHONEMES AND GRAPHEMES

No doubt the most debilitating factor in learning to read, write, and spell is that, in most cases, there is not a consistent one-to-one relationship between the letter (grapheme) and the sound the letter makes (phoneme). The alphabet has only twenty-six graphemes, yet there are at least forty phonemes. By actual count, English is fourteen letters short, but really the deficiency is more like seventeen, since three of the letters (*c, q,* and *x*) are redundant in that they repeat sounds symbolized by other letters. English gets around this problem of not enough letters to represent the phonemes of the language in two ways: First, it uses two or more letters in combinations to create digraphs (e.g., *th, ng, oi, oo, eigh, ough*), or, second, one letter can serve for more than one sound (e.g., *a = fat, father, any, what; o = love, move, wolf, woman*).

Taking all these factors into account, the child just beginning to learn to read soon finds out that learning the alphabet and the sounds of the letters is quite a bundle. Mario Pei, in *The Story of the English Language* (1967, p. 338), sums it up this way: "[O]ur spelling is more than irrational—it is inhuman and forms the bane not merely of foreigners, but of our own younger generations, compelled to devote interminable hours to learning a system which is the soul and essence of anarchy."

THE SOUNDS OF ENGLISH

Figure 2.1 is a listing of the major phoneme and grapheme correspondences (sound to symbol relationships) and shows examples of the various spellings of a single phoneme that regularly appear in print. The percentages that appear in parentheses after some spellings indicate the number of times, or frequency, a particular variation of the spelling was used to represent its corresponding phoneme in a study of the seventeen thousand most frequently used words in English (Hanna, Hanna, Hodge, & Rudolph, 1966). Percentages are given for the highest-frequency spellings.

It must be pointed out that since phonemes represent sounds and sounds differ according to stress, accents, dialects, and other factors, linguists do not always agree on the exact number of phonemes. Generally, most authorities conclude that English has at least forty to forty-four phonemes.

When he or she learns to count, a child's logic is not impeded. The first twelve numbers require memorization, but once the teen numbers are reached, a rational and consistent way of counting and numbering persists and makes it easy to carry that process into the 20s, 30s, 40s, and on into the hundreds and thousands ad infinitum. But what if learning arithmetic was as confusing a process as learning to read? Imagine how much more difficult learning to count would be if a student had to deal with the concept of lowercase numbers and uppercase numbers, manuscript numbers and cursive numbers, long numbers and short numbers, compound numbers, number demons, contracted numbers, and numbers that were entirely different in value but were pronounced the same. To carry the analogy one step further, imagine how frustrating it could be to learn to add or subtract the simplest of numbers if numbers changed their value depending on the position in a configuration, as happens with alphabetical symbols. If these kinds of inconsistencies and misdirection happened with our arithmetic symbols, we might have fewer math majors around, and perhaps fewer modern inventions and conveniences as well.

THE GOOD NEWS ABOUT ENGLISH ORTHOGRAPHY

Looking at the difficulties of English spelling, with all those multiple spellings for phonemes, one might be tempted to agree with Mario Pei. But now that we've glimpsed the dark side, let's explore the bright side of English spelling. Looking closely, one can begin to see the silver lining. One study (Furness, 1990), for example, showed that in a sampling of three thousand basic words, 85 percent are spelled with complete regularity— that is, each sound is spelled with the same letter, or letters, in every word every time it appears. Prior to that study, researchers (Hanna et al., 1966) received a government grant to attempt to determine just how phonemic English spelling is. They programmed a computer with all the phonemic spelling rules they knew of and had the computer apply the rules to seventeen thousand of the most common words in English. Except in cases of human error in programming, the computer managed to spell almost all the words correctly.

When the language is viewed beyond just the surface structure, it becomes apparent that a sense of order and logic exists in the various ways in which words are written. The vast majority of the alternative spellings for individual phonemes, for example, affect only a very limited number of words, and, excluding these, each phoneme usually has just one or two principal representations. And even when these rarer spellings are encountered (kind, mind, find; night, fight, tight; cold, fold, hold), a certain consistency in their spelling pattern makes them easier to remember. In addition, it is rare to find more than one irregular spelling in these words. Many words with the less frequent spellings (nonphonemic spellings) can be either taught later, when students' skills are more developed, or taught as sight words.

Figure 2.1 Phoneme-Grapheme Spelling Patterns

Consonants:

Phoneme	Key word	Alternative Spellings
/**b**/	**b**ed	<u>b</u>ike (97%), bu<u>bb</u>le, ras<u>p</u>berry, ro<u>be</u>
/**ch**/	**ch**est	<u>ch</u>urch (55%), <u>c</u>ello (31%), wa<u>tch</u>, ma<u>t</u>ure, <u>Cz</u>ech, bes<u>ti</u>al, righ<u>te</u>ous
/**d**/	**d**esk	<u>d</u>id (96%), wing<u>ed</u>, la<u>dd</u>er, woul<u>d</u>
/**f**/	**f**un	<u>f</u>at (78%), o<u>ff</u>, <u>ph</u>onics, rou<u>gh</u>, wi<u>fe</u>, sa<u>pph</u>ire, o<u>ft</u>en
/**g**/	**g**un	<u>g</u>et (88%), e<u>gg</u>, <u>gh</u>ost, <u>g</u>uest, e<u>x</u>it

/h/	hen	home (98%), whose, Mojave
/dz/	jump	joy (66%), wedge, goal, pigeon, religion, suggest, judgment, soldier, grandeur, vision
/k/	king	came (73%), sick, account, monarch, walk, acquire, chorus, except, ache, saccharine, school, biscuit, ecstasy, liquor
/l/	love	look (91%), tall, pale
/m/	must	make (94%), bomb, mummy, autumn, phlegm
/n/	nest	not (97%), know, inn, gnat, pneumatic
/ng/	sing	song, tongue
/p/	post	pet (96%), happy, shepherd, hope, hiccough
/r/	run	rub (97%), sorry, corps, myrrh, write, mortgage, rhythm
/s/	sun	six (73%), city, face, mass, science, schism, sword, psalm, fasten, vase
/sh/	ship	shop (26%), partial, ocean, musician, sure, prescient, mansion, anxious
/t/	tent	test (97%), mitten, thyme, doubt, indict, late, two, talked
/th/	thin	thirst (100%)
/th/	the	there (100%)
/v/	vase	voice (99.5%), of, save, Stephen
/w/	we	won (92%), one
/wh/	when	wheat (100%)
/z/	zoo	hers (64%), zing
/zh/	treasure	division (44%), measure, barrage
/y/	you	yes (89%), onion, hallelujah

(Continued)

(Continued)

Vowels:

Phoneme	Key word	Alternative Spellings
/ă/	cat	fact (96%), have, plaid, laugh, calf
/ā/	take	table (43%), mail, way, great, rein, eight, grey, gauge, straight, champagne, suede, forte, they
/âr/	care	fare (23%) pair, prayer, there, pear, their
/ä/	father	father (89%), rot, heart, knowledge, haul, alms
/ĕ/	let	bend (91%), bread, any, said, says, heifer, friend, bury, leopard
/ē/	me	be (70%), heat, seize, people, key, suite, antique, Caesar, mosquito, piano, city
/ĭ/	tin	ship (66%), hymn (23%), women, busy, built, give, been, village, minute, mountain, forfeit, marriage
/ī/	find	bind (37%), try, aisle, aye, I, lie, eye, align, right, buy, rye, height
/îr/	fear	tear, here, beer, weird, pier
/ŏ/	hop	not (79%), wash, yacht, sausage, gone, knowledge, honest
/ō/	no	go (73%), home, coarse, oh, goat, crow, toe, folks, soul, sew, though, owe, yeoman, depot, rogue
/ô/	ball	fall, talk, Utah, warm, daughter, haunt, paw, order, thought, broad, brawl
/oi/	boil/toy	boil (62%), boy (32%), buoy, noise
/ou/	house	mouse (57%), hour, bough, now
/oo/	look	took (31%), bush (51%), wolf, should
/ōō/	boot	toot (38%), rule (21%), flew, canoe, through, blue, fruit, coupe, lieutenant, maneuver
/ū/	but	cut (86%), blood, does, money, some, tongue, rubbed, couple

/yo͞o/	you	<u>u</u>se (69%), b<u>eau</u>ty, f<u>eu</u>d, d<u>eu</u>ce, f<u>ew</u>, cl<u>ue</u>, adi<u>eu</u>, h<u>u</u>man, q<u>ueue</u>, <u>you</u>, <u>yu</u>le, s<u>ui</u>t
/ûr/	st<u>er</u>n	f<u>er</u>n (40%), b<u>ir</u>d, w<u>or</u>k, j<u>our</u>ney, m<u>yr</u>tle, m<u>yrr</u>h
/ə/ schwa	<u>a</u>gain	<u>a</u>dept, synth<u>e</u>sis, dec<u>i</u>mal, medi<u>u</u>m, s<u>y</u>ringe

SOURCE: Percentages from Hanna, P. R., Hanna, J. L., Hodge, R. F., & Rudolph, E. H. (1966). *Phoneme-grapheme correspondence as clues to spelling improvement*. Washington, DC: U.S. Office of Education.

GETTING BEYOND THE SURFACE STRUCTURE OF ENGLISH

Let us take a closer look at alternative spellings of phonemes in greater detail to discern the consistency that can be found. Our daily language is filled with examples of this consistency.

Consonants: In the consonant phonemes in Figure 2.1, the reader might note that, with the exception of *c* and *g*, generally one consistent spelling of the sound appears most often. For example, the predominant spelling for most consonants is a single letter—*b* = *b* (97%); *n* = *n* (97%); *p* = *p* (96%); *r* = *r* (97%) (Blevins, 1998; Hanna et al., 1966).

Another common spelling is doubling a consonant (i.e., *rubber, inn, happen, marry*).

Trying to decide whether the consonant is spelled with a single or double letter may cause problems in working out how to spell a word, but the two spellings do not misdirect pronunciation while reading. *Rubber* and *ruber, inn* and *in,* and *marry* and *Mary* are pronounced the same in either spelling. Although spelling these words with a single consonant would be a mistake in spelling, it would not cause a miscue in reading. The few variations beyond these two spellings generally involve the presence of silent consonants, which are fairly consistent themselves (see p. 26), or other letters that do not cause serious pronunciation problems.

The two other consonants *c* and *g*, both of which have two different sounds, are also quite consistent and easily learned by students. For example, when c is followed by *e, i,* or *y* (*cease, city, cyst,* etc.) it has the "soft" sound usually associated with *s*. When *c* is followed by *a, o,* or *u*, it has the "hard" sound usually associated with *k* (*cat, course, custom,* etc.). When *c* follows a short vowel it is generally spelled with a *ck* (*sick, clock, duck,* etc.). It seems safe to conclude, then, that the relationship between consonant phonemes and graphemes, although not always perfectly consistent, is close enough to be reliable and valuable for instruction. The same conclusion may be valid for consonant blends, as approximately 82 percent of consonant blends are spelled regularly (Furness, 1990).

Vowels: The various spellings for the same vowel sound can be most confusing and frustrating at times. Yet, even with the vowels' spelling patterns, a great deal of consistency exists. In most cases, a reader can arrive at the exact or approximate pronunciation of a vowel sound from the way a word is written. Short vowels are especially reliable. Usually, when a single vowel is found in a word, as is shown in Figure 2.1, it is short—*a* = *cat* (96%), *e* = *end* (91%), *i* = *tin* and *y* = *hymn* (89%), ***o*** = ***not*** (79%), *u* = *cut* (86%) (Blevins, 1998; Hanna et al., 1966). Long vowels generally are indicated by vowel digraphs or by a silent e at the end of the word. Within these two generalizations, the spelling of long vowels is also fairly consistent. Usually, the vowel digraphs are *ai* and *ay* (*maid, say*) for the long /a/; *ee* and *ea* (*keep* and *reach*) for the long /e/; *ie* and final *y* (*tried, sky*) for the long /i/; *oa, oe,* and *ow* (*boat, toe, show*) for the long /o/; and *ue* and *ew* (*blue, threw*) for the long /u/. When the *y* is found at the end of a one-syllable word (*try, my, sky*, etc.), it is always pronounced as a long /i/. When *y* is at the end of a multisyllabic word or is used as an adverbial ending, it has the sound of the long /e/ (*handy, funny, windy, nicely,* etc.).

Diphthongs and Vowel Digraphs: These elements of English spelling are also fairly consistent. In dipthongs *oi–oy* and *ou–ow,* for example, the *oi* sound as in *oil* and *boil* and the *oy* sound as in *boy* and *joy* are represented by two different spellings, yet both spellings are consistent. Upon examination, it is noted that the *oi* spelling most often appears in a closed syllable (inside the word) with words such as *toil, coin, voice;* and the *oy* spelling appears as an open syllable (at the end) with *boy, ploy, soy,* etc. The same thing is true of the dipthongs *ou–ow.* There are two spellings for one sound. As in the previous examples, the spelling *ou* (*house, mouse, blouse,* etc.) is generally within the word, and the spelling *ow* (*how, now, cow,* etc.) is generally at the end of the word. The same is true for the digraphs *au* and *aw.* Generally, the *au* spelling appears in a closed syllable (*daughter, Paul, autumn,* etc.), and *aw* is found at the end of a word (*saw, claw, straw,* etc.).

Silent Letters: Although most silent letters in English serve little purpose other than to confuse and misdirect reading and spelling, they do, nonetheless, have a certain consistency and order about them, so that they cause little difficulty for an advanced reader and speller. Notice that although the letters are silent, they are generally located at the same spot in the word and with the same neighboring letters (see Figure 2.2).

Figure 2.2   Silent Letters and Their Positions

silent a	silent b	silent d	silent g	silent gh
head	bomb	edge	gnat	fight
learn	climb	ledge	gnome	light
bread	comb	fudge	gnu	right
deaf	lamb	hedge	gnaw	sight

silent k	silent 1	silent h	silent t	silent w
knock	half	hour	soften	write
knit	calf	honor	often	wrong
know	palms	ghastly	castle	wrist
knife	calm	ghost	bustle	wrap

LACK OF BARRIERS TO READING COMPREHENSION

One thing to remember is that even though reading and spelling are considered opposite sides of the same coin (one side is decoding, the other encoding), they are not the same as far as ease of learning goes. When children are learning to read and do not immediately recognize the word, they can use the letters to "sound out" the word and finally figure it out. The word *sneeze*, for example, could just as easily be written as *sneese*, *snease*, *sneaze*, *sneize*, or *sneaze*, and it would still be pronounced the same with the same meaning.

In some ways, the irregularity of spelling can be an aid in sight reading because it helps students learn words as configurations rather than sounds. Many young learners, for example, learn to read many high-frequency words such as *does, was, the, love*, etc., before they come to school or have learned anything about letter sounds. They learn to read these words not by the process of sounding them out, but, rather, by a natural and untaught process of simply recognizing them as the regular and "normal" representation. As children learn to read more and more words, they increasingly repress the sounds and begin to look at words more for their meaning. Learning and experiencing various spellings of the same sounds in words, the children are better able to recognize words at a more advanced stage, getting sounds and meaning simultaneously.

In reading, getting to the exact pronunciation of a word is not as important as getting to the exact spelling is in the writing process. The general context of the sentence, paragraph, and story helps guide the student to the right pronunciation. If young readers encounter the sentence "Father parked his car in the garage" and are having a hard time figuring out what "garage" means, they can get close enough to the pronunciation by trying to sound it out. A good chance exists that by the process of trying to sound it out in the context of the total sentence, the reader will come close enough to the exact pronunciation to eventually get it right. If all else fails, the reader can often figure out the meaning of the strange word using the words around it and the sense of the sentence. In the example, the reader can try to sound out the word and/or the reason that the place where one parks a car is a garage.

The bottom line is that while variations in how words are written are a cause of concern and frustration at times, they are not necessarily a barrier to reading comprehension.

ORDER OF TEACHING PHONOLOGICAL SKILLS

As students, even in the same grade or age level, have widely differing reading abilities, it is difficult to determine the exact order in which a particular skill ought to be taught for each student. About all that can be said is that, generally, or for the average student at least, most phonics instruction will be completed by the end of the third grade or beginning of the fourth. On the other hand, it must be pointed out that the more complicated concepts, such as the meaning of particular prefixes and suffixes and the segmentation of longer words, often continue to be taught in the later elementary grades and beyond. For purposes of remediation, much of the content of phonetic instruction may be reviewed, or learned, at a later grade level—including adult education programs, if necessary.

Since all learning should be geared to meeting individual or classroom needs, it's impossible to set out an exact order or sequence for teaching phonics in all cases. In theory, however, there is a logical and desirable procedure that starts with the most familiar and goes on to the less familiar, or that proceeds from the simpler to the more complex. Provided students have already developed a satisfactory degree of skill in auditory and visual discrimination and have learned to recognize at least a few basic sight words, the following order of presenting phonological awareness is suggested.

(For a complete summary of the phonological skills taught for reading and spelling, see Resource B.)

Phonological Sequencing of Instruction

    A. Consonants: "closed-mouth" sounds; letters of the alphabet that are not vowels

        1. Consonants that have one main sound (*b, d, f, h, j, k, l, m, n, p, q (u), r, t, v, w, y, z*)

2. Consonants that have two sounds (*c*, *g*, and *s*)

3. Ending consonant sounds

4. Phonograms: letter groupings that have the same sound in many words, usually a vowel sound plus a consonant sound that, added to a consonant or blend, make a new word (*-ake: take, make, lake,* etc.; *-ang: sang, rang, clang,* etc.)

5. Consonant digraphs: two consecutive consonants that form a single unique sound (*ch, gh, ph (f), sh, th, wh*)

6. Consonant blends: two or three consecutive consonants that form a new blended sound (initial blends: *bl, cl, fl, gl, pl, sl, br, cr, dr, fr, gr, pr, tr, sc, sk, sl, sm, sn, sp, st, sw, dw, sw, tw, scr, shr, squ, spl, str, thr;* ending blends: *-bl, -ct, -ft, -ld, -lf, -lk, -lm, -lp, -lt, -mp, -nc, -nch, -nd, -ng, -nk, -nt, -pl, -pt, -rd, -rg, -rk, -rl, -rm, -rn, -rs, -rt, -sk, -sp, -st, -tl*)

7. Silent consonants: consonants that are not heard in certain words or combinations of letters (*duck, sign, honest, high,* etc.)

B. Vowels: "opened-mouth" letters of the alphabet that are not consonants. The letters *a, e, i, o,* and *u* are always vowels. *W* and *y* produce vowel sounds when they follow another vowel (*law, new, how; say, key, toy,* etc.). When y is the only vowel in a word (*try, my, sky,* etc.) or the only vowel in a syllable (*funny, July, mystery,* etc.), then it is a vowel.

1. Short vowel sounds: vowels that are low in tone and take a short time to pronounce

2. Long vowel sounds: vowels that are high in tone and take a longer time to pronounce

3. Rules for determining whether a vowel is long or short

4. R-controlled vowels: a vowel followed by *r;* has a special sound different from the one usually associated with that vowel (*her, corn, girl, fur,* etc.)

5. Vowel digraphs: two vowels together that produce one vowel sound (*leaf, foe, build, piece, zoom,* etc.)

6. Vowel diphthongs: formed when two vowels come together to produce a new single sound unlike short or long vowel sounds (*boy, join, cow, proud, snow,* etc.)

7. Miscellaneous vowel sounds (*moon, shoot, book, cause, salt, candy,* etc.)

C. Syllabication: dividing words into syllables in order to sound out the words

1. Rules for dividing words into syllables (V stands for vowel; C stands for consonant):

      a. VC-CV: *rab-bit, tor-ment, pret-zel, let-ter, suf-fix,* etc.

      b. V-CV: *ma-jor, be-gin, lo-cal, ba-by, po-lice,* etc.

      c. VC-V: *doz-en, lem-on, col-or, riv-er, hab-it,* etc.

      d. *–ble*: final syllable constituted by the endings *-ble, -cle, -dle, -gle, -kle, -ple, -tle, and -zle*

2. Prefixes and suffixes: syllables placed at the beginning and ending of words to change their meaning, generally counted as syllables by themselves and, as such, excluded from the syllables of the root word (*un-fit, re-do, poor-ly, good-ness,* etc.)

3. Compound words: two words together that form a new word (*sunshine, butterfly, moonlight, football,* etc.)

4. Contractions: shortened forms of two words written as one (*I'd, can't, don't, it's, you'll,* etc.)

5. Inflectional endings: additions to the end of a word to change time or tense of a verb (*look, looks, looked*), or the quantity (number) of a noun (*boy–boys, glove–gloves, rose–roses,* etc.)

CONCLUSION

It would be like living in an educational dream world if English orthography were as consistent as Portuguese, Italian, German, and most other languages where a greater conformity exists between sound and symbol, or phoneme and grapheme.

Wouldn't it be wonderful, if after students had learned the symbols and sounds, they were able to pronounce each word they see with one hundred percent accuracy? There would be no need for the varied and innovative methods that have been created over the years. Just teach the letter sounds and students will, with a minimum of practice, automatically learn to pronounce words. No more memorization of generalizations, no more repetitive drills or exercises, no more stumbling over words.

After such wishful dreaming comes the reality that the student and teacher must deal with English the way it is, not the way they wish it were. The reality, however, isn't all that bad. English orthography, or the way words are written and spelled, isn't perfect—in fact, it's far from it—but it doesn't have to be perfect to be learned. The system has a great deal of consistency and logic and, if presented correctly, it can be easily learned by almost every student in the elementary grades.

It is because of all the intricacies of English that the teacher must use a variety of approaches and techniques to get the lesson across. It is because of these intricacies that reading classes should never be boring or routine.

The good news is that, although English writing may be more difficult to encode than other orthographies, it has some benefits that other more structured orthographies do not. For example, English is not encumbered with whole sets of conjugations, declensions, and inflectional endings that so challenge learners of other languages. English has no prescribed word order, so there is greater freedom and variety of expression. English not only has the largest vocabulary of any language in the world, a single word can have dozens of different meanings depending on its use in the sentence. English is the language of navigation, aviation, television, commerce, and the movies. It is the second language of many countries of the world and the closest thing we have to an international language.

English has so many good things going for it that the sometimes annoying repetitions young learners have to put up with when learning to read are well worth it.

3

Teaching
the Alphabet

Many children ages two, three, and four must feel as if they live in a world of letters. The boy next door, whom I'll call Blake, is one of these. The walls of his bedroom are decorated with large multicolored letters of various sizes and shapes. In the center of his bedroom hangs a huge ABC mobile, which glows in the dark. Next to the nightstand lies his ABC telephone, which toots its approval when the proper letter button is pushed. Scattered in the middle of the room and into the far corners are groupings of alphabet blocks. In the bookcase, we see alphabet books of all sizes and colors. And when nature calls, it's off to the alphabet-ringed potty chair. And how many times has Blake been paraded out to sing the "elemeno" song, not only for family, but also for everyone else within earshot? All these modern conveniences are provided by Blake's progressive father for the worthy purpose of making sure Blake gets off to a good start in school.

For every Blake, however, an equal number of children come to school with little or no exposure to books or reading material. One study, for example, pointed out that 60 percent of the youngsters who did poorly in school didn't own a single book (Feitelson & Goldstein, 1986). Another study showed that while the typical middle-class child enters first grade with approximately one thousand hours of being read to, children from lower-income families average just twenty-five hours (Adams, 1998). And at every income level and in every type of family situation, one encounters children who are encouraged to sit passively in front of the television for hours a day. This does not bode well for getting off to a good start in reading.

Kindergarten and first grade classrooms are a composite of boys and girls, ranging from those who are highly motivated and eager to learn to those who have no motivation at all. "They come to school with literacy experiences that range from zero to 2,000 hours" (California Department of Education, 1996, p. 19). Some come already able to read at the primer level; others can't tell one letter from another. Some children can write many words from memory using lowercase letters; others are not sure how to hold a pencil. All these very fragile youngsters—those who are well prepared and those who are not—will need special handling, inspiration, and role modeling by the teacher. The task of getting all these children off to a good start is the tremendous challenge of the kindergarten or first grade teacher, and one that will more than likely determine the child's educational future. More than anything else, the child's engagement and participation in learning will be dependent on the atmosphere—the momentum, support, and expectations—created by their first classroom teachers (Adams, 1998, commenting on Chall's 1967 study of over 300 classrooms). For this reason alone, there are no more important teachers than the ones who start it all.

WHY LEARNING THE ALPHABET IS IMPORTANT

English, like Spanish, German, and most of the other major languages of the world, is an alphabetical language. The letters of the alphabet are abstract symbols, made up of various forms and shapes that stand for the sounds of the language. When these symbols are written together, they form written or printed words. When they are read together, they form spoken words. The manner in which words are consistently written enables a relationship to be established between the visual capacities of readers and their auditory and oral capacities. The manner in which words are consistently spelled allows one person to communicate with another through the written word. Learning the letters and sounds of the alphabet and then being able to use them in written communications is one of the bases upon which an educated society is predicated.

Learning the alphabet is the first formal step in education. It has always been considered the school's most important task and the foundation of all the other subjects in school (Smith, 1986). This fact has been recognized from earliest times. In colonial days, for example, every child entering school had to memorize the stanza below.

He who will never learn his ABC

Will forever a blockhead be. (Gray, 1963, p. 45)

Although you would never hear the verse in classrooms today, it does hold a grain of truth. If students fail to learn the alphabet, they won't have much chance to go very far in education. They may not "a blockhead be" but they certainly will feel like one. Until children learn the form and shape of individual letters, they cannot begin to start reading or writing words. Until children learn the individual sounds of the letters, they will have difficulty with more involved aspects of reading. Research indicates that the single best predictor of early success in reading is accurate, rapid identification of the upper- and lowercase letters of the alphabet. The second-best indicator is phonemic awareness—the awareness of smaller units of sound within spoken words (Adams, 1998). In three key language-arts areas—reading, spelling, and writing—knowledge and mastery of the alphabet is the prerequisite for achievement and success.

In its reading initiative publication, *Teaching Reading*, the California State Board of Education recognizes the value of learning the alphabet as a first step in learning to read. It states:

- Until children can quickly recognize letters, they cannot begin to appreciate that all words are made up of sequences and patterns of letters.
- Until children can comfortably discriminate the shape of one letter from another, there is no point in teaching letter-sound pairings.
- Knowledge of the letter names is important for it has been shown to be a major means by which children recall or generate sounds of letters in their independent reading and writing. (California State Board of Education, 1996, p. 5)

The California report goes on to stress that since the names and shapes of the letters are similar to each other, learning them is best fostered through playful exposure to the alphabet. It also encourages preschool and kindergarten teachers to expose their students to names, shapes, and formation of the letters of the alphabet (California State Board of Education, 1996).

DIFFICULTIES OF LEARNING THE LETTERS

Learning the symbol system doesn't come naturally to children. They must learn the names of the letters in order and out of order, associate sounds to the letters, write the letters, put the letters together to form words, and put the words into sentences. Although many children come to school able to sing the "Alphabet Song," write some of the letters of the alphabet, and read a few words, kindergarten will not necessarily be easy for them. There is so much more to learning the alphabet than mere recitation.

Learning the alphabet is difficult for many students for two principal reasons. In the first place, kindergarten students are just learning how to learn and may not be ready to process the vast amount of new knowledge and experiences to which they have suddenly become exposed. The second reason is the complexities and inconsistencies of the alphabet itself.

The Shapes and Forms of Letters

When children enter school, so much is expected of them. In addition to learning the forms of the letters, they will need extra practice distinguishing letters that have similar forms or shapes. Children have already learned to recognize things by their size and shape. A car is a car whether it is viewed from the front or back. A book is a book whether it's upside down or not. When it comes to learning the letters, however, new perceptions are necessary. When the d is turned, it becomes a b; when the M is upside down, it becomes a W. Many subtle changes in letters also make them difficult to distinguish one from the other. The lowercase b and d often are confused with the lowercase a if the horizontal line of the a is not tall enough. The lowercase g and q, m and n, and a and o are also often difficult to distinguish and are sometimes confused one for the other. The uppercase letters T, E, and F also have identification problems. When the student learns cursive handwriting in a year or two, again there will be another long period of transition when words are often spelled or written with a mixture of the manuscript and cursive forms. Often this mixture lasts into adult life and becomes the normal or usual way of writing.

Learning the alphabet for some students represents the same level of difficulty as an adult attempting to learn Chinese for the first time. Unlike with Chinese—one of the few nonalphabetic languages—children soon learn that with English there are at least four different ways in which individual letters can be represented or written. The first two ways are the uppercase and lowercase manuscript letters, and then some time later, the upper- and lowercase cursive letters. The word *the,* for example, can be written or viewed in the following ways: THE, The, the. When one considers all the different typefaces and the wide variety in styles of handwriting, making out individual letters and words can become a confusing task, especially for children who may not have had experience or exposure to all the variations. It seems logical to conclude that when the visual patterns presented to children are inconsistent and confusing, chances are very good that they will have a more difficult time in forming the necessary associations between the sound and symbol as well.

New Ideas and Concepts

Overcoming these kinds of confusing problems regarding the forms and shapes of letters is only the beginning, however. Once students get over these novel aspects of learning the letters, they are slowly introduced to a whole set of other new ideas and concepts about letters that also must be learned and mastered. Here are a few of them:

- In reality, fifty-two (not twenty-six) letters have to be learned, considering each letter has two forms—uppercase (capital) and lowercase. It is no help to discover that some of the lowercase letters are smaller versions of the uppercase letters (*C—c, V—v, X—x*), while most of the lowercase letters have no resemblance to their uppercase forms (*D—d, E—e, G—g*).
- The upper- and lowercase forms are not interchangeable. Sometimes only small letters must be used while at other times a capital letter

is required. To put an uppercase letter where a lowercase one is required, or vice versa, is a misspelling.

- There are two types of letters—vowels and consonants. Both have different functions in words. Vowels are further divided into long and short, with no sure way of telling the difference from appearance and position alone.
- Each form of the letter must be remembered in order and identified out of order.
- Letters stand for sounds, but the sounds can vary as words vary.
- Letters make up words, and words make up sentences.

After having spent hours and hours learning the manuscript alphabet, students must then turn around and learn a totally new way of writing the alphabet in another year or two.

Is it any wonder, then, that so many children have such a difficult time learning and retaining necessary information about the alphabet? This is especially true since so many of them have little or no preschool training or experience with identifying and writing the letters. The problems are even greater and more involved when so many children are entering school with almost no knowledge of, and little experience with, speaking English.

When students enter the kindergarten room for the first time they find it to be, like Blake's bedroom, full of reminders of just how important the alphabet is. Large colorful alphabet cards usually line the front of the room. Alphabet picture books are often found on the bookshelf. Among their everyday activities, students learn to sing, dance, and clap to the alphabet. They learn to point to the letters, trace the letters, cut out the letters, color the letters, arrange the letters, and write the letters. Kindergarten teachers often read book after book and use trick after trick to help all their students learn the letters of the alphabet, as well as good listening and reading skills.

Following up on the efforts of the kindergarten teacher, the first grade teacher uses another bag of tricks to ensure that students master the sounds of the letters by creating opportunities and activities for them to further develop their alphabetical skills. After two years of this kind of exposure, if a student is still having difficulty with learning the alphabet, additional activities and workbook exercises on the sounds of the letters are reinforced and reviewed over and over again in the second and third grades—and beyond, if necessary. It is safe to say that probably more time and energy are spent teaching the alphabet than on any other single endeavor in school.

Yet, despite all the time, effort, and emphasis placed on teaching the alphabet, it is amazing the number of second graders, fifth graders, and even high school students who cannot recite all the letters in proper order, associate sounds with letters, or write all the letters of the alphabet. It is discouraging how many upper elementary students, despite all previous efforts to the contrary, still reverse letters, confuse one letter with another, or mix manuscript and cursive letters together. I myself have confronted this situation repeatedly over years of teaching reading. One of the most baffling questions some early elementary teachers must ask themselves is why, despite all their efforts, so many children fail to learn or retain fundamental knowledge of the alphabet. Times have changed, that's true. It is also true that children and their attitudes have changed. But the urgent need to know and master the alphabet has not changed—that remains the more essential truth. The challenge is to find ways to ensure that all children in school learn and master the alphabet.

Attempts to Change the Alphabet

It is precisely because of the peculiar difficulties of the English alphabet that scholars, writers, lexicographers, and statesmen such as Benjamin Franklin, Noah Webster, Isaac Pitman, George Bernard Shaw, and many others over the centuries have made proposals to change the alphabet in some degree or another (Starrett, 1981).

Many educators over the years have devised systems to make it easier for students to decode words. In 1960, for example, Helen Bonnema, a high school principal in Denver, Colorado, invented a system for prereading instruction in kindergarten and first grade. The system, among other things, used phonetic respelling of many words (*kwik–quick, hed–head, lau–law*) and used diacritical marks to denote long vowels (kē, plā, gōst, jū). She added the inverted e (ə) for the schwa sound (Bonnema, 1961). Harry Lindgren, president of the Action Spelling Society (headquartered in Australia), in 1969, advocated using spelling changes and diacritical marks to indicate vowel length. Several books were published with many of his changes (Starrett, 1981).

Other educators have resorted to colors to indicate vowel sounds. One of the earliest attempts appeared in the *Dale Readers* at the turn of the twentieth century. The color-coding system that received the greatest amount of notoriety was *Words in Color* by Caleb Gattegno in 1962. Gattegno believed that 280 signs would be needed to represent the forty-seven sounds of English. Instead of using new signs or symbols, he chose to use distinct colors to represent these sounds because the colors "would not disturb the shape of the image which the words create in the mind of the learner" (Gattegno, 1962, p. 2).

The most famous reading program using an augmented alphabet was the Initial Teaching Alphabet (i. t. a.) of British spelling reformer Sir James Pitman. The alphabet contained forty-five characters or symbols to represent the forty-five phonemes of English. They were all written in one form so that capital letters were merely larger forms of the small letters. Digraphs were written as one letter, both in spacing and shape. This alphabet was not intended as a permanent reform, but was used in the initial stages of reading to assist students in learning. Once students gained fluency in reading, they were gradually introduced to standard spellings of words. Pitman's system gained wide recognition and success in the United Kingdom.

In 1963, i/ t/ a (the addition of virgules to the name helped to distinguish it from the English version) was introduced in the United States in Bethlehem, Pennsylvania. The reading program consisted of a series of seven books, or readers, written with i/t/a symbols (identical to the British symbols) but with stories and ideas that would appeal to American beginning readers. The i/t/a/ symbols were introduced gradually and were used in conjunction with a language arts approach to reading with activities in reading, handwriting, creative writing, spelling, and thinking. The last book in the series was a combination of i/t/a/ and traditional spelling and was meant to assist students in reading in traditional orthography (Mazurkiewicz, & Tanyzer, 1966). This program spread rather quickly. In a few years, over three thousand students in seven states were using i/t/a in the initial stages of reading. The evaluations were somewhat mixed, and i/t/a soon died from lack of enthusiasm (Starrett, 1981).

Although good intentions and great ingenuity have abounded, so far nobody has invented an alternate English alphabet that has found broad acceptance. It seems as though for the moment we must accept our challenging orthography as it is and concentrate on finding the most effective ways to teach it to children.

THE IMPORTANCE OF MEANINGFUL PRACTICE AND REPETITION

For most students, the arduous task of learning the forms and sounds of the letters takes a great deal of individual attention, repetition, and practice. The need for repetition and practice, however, doesn't mean simply doing the task over the same way every time, with the implied message: "You'll sit here all day until you get it right!" It simply means that parents and educators have to use different means and activities—or whatever it takes to make learning and mastering the alphabet as meaningful and rewarding as possible. Variety, with a little bit of patience and praise thrown into the mix, can go a long way toward making repetitive tasks rewarding for the teacher and student.

The Guide to the California Reading Initiative of 1996 points out several important considerations teachers ought to be aware of when teaching the alphabet. It suggests the following:

- Teach upper- and lowercase letters separately.
- Begin with uppercase letters in preschool. Since the ability to read lowercase letters is more important for teaching reading text, it may be wiser to emphasize lowercase letters when working with first graders who have a little letter knowledge.

- Incorporate printing into instruction about letters as a powerful means of developing letter recognition.
- Use letter/keyword/picture displays when introducing letter-sound instruction. (California State Board of Education, 1996)

WHEN TO REMEDIATE

One thing that must be remembered is that most reading problems don't begin in the second or third grade. Most reading problems have their origin much earlier—in preschool and kindergarten. Formal reading instruction begins with learning the alphabet and how to reproduce the letters, and associating sounds with these letters. If for some reason the students don't learn the names of the letters or cannot associate sounds with letters, they will not have much success with other facets of reading. Getting off to a good start in reading builds up a student's confidence and eagerness to attempt more advanced learning. Confidence is the name of the game when it comes to reading and most other aspects of life. Students who have no confidence in their reading endeavors will start to fall further and further behind.

One of the criteria for remedial reading programs in the past was that the student had to be at least two grade levels behind before he or she could receive special help. This meant most programs were filled with fourth, fifth, and sixth graders. In many cases, it was too little too late. Research indicates that if schools delay intervention programs until age seven, 75 percent of remedial students will continue to have difficulties. If reading problems are identified as early as the first or second grade they can be remedied 82 percent of the time. On the other hand, if the school waits until third, fourth, or fifth grade to intervene, the problems can be remedied only 46 percent of the time (Adams, 1998). In other words, early identification of reading problems and subsequent intervention is almost twice as effective as later identification and intervention.

Fortunately, today, school districts have recognized the need for early intervention. Students who are at risk of failing to read are now identified in kindergarten and first grade and given special help before their reading problems have reached the critical stages. The Reading Task Force in California emphasizes the need for early intervention: "Schools must have an effective, rigorous, proven intervention program as part of their comprehensive literacy plan for instruction, with emphasis on early intervention for children by mid-first grade" (California Department of Education, 1996, p. 20).

ACTIVITIES FOR TEACHING THE ALPHABET

There are many profitable ways of involving young children in activities for learning to identify the names, shapes, and sounds of the alphabet.

The very best source for learning just what ideas and activities are most effective is to talk to the real experts: experienced classroom teachers. If they have been around for a while, they generally have a wealth of ideas and love to share them with other teachers. Below are some of the popular activities teachers use to assist students in learning the alphabet.

Alphabet Song

Since so many children already come to school knowing how to sing the "Alphabet Song," this is a good place to get them all started. Let those who know the song teach it to those who do not. Once the students learn the song, several additional activities fit in nicely and can be incorporated into the song.

Write the letters of the alphabet on the blackboard. As the students sing the song, have one student volunteer to point to the individual letters as each is mentioned.

Make large (9" × 12") letters of the alphabet out of construction paper or poster board. On one side is the uppercase letter; on the other side is the lowercase letter. Mix up the cards and pass them out to members of the class. As the song is sung, have the students hold up their respective letters as each one is named.

Make large (9" × 12") letters of the alphabet out of construction paper or poster board. Mix up the letters and pass them out to members of the class. As the song is sung slowly (very slowly at first), have the student with the first letter run to the front of the room; as B is mentioned, have the student with that letter come forward and stand next to A, and so on. This activity will probably cause lots of confusion, especially at the beginning, but it also causes much laughter and enjoyment. Not recommended for teachers who require a lot of order and formality.

Alphabet Box

Each student is asked to find a small plastic container with a top, or a small box the size of a half-pint milk carton. For each student in the class, the teacher reproduces the alphabet on twenty-six 1" × 1.5" construction paper or poster board rectangles with the lowercase letters on one side and the corresponding uppercase letters on the other. These alphabet boxes can be used for a variety of purposes, including identifying vowels and consonants, making simple words, making simple sentences, and providing examples of letters to be copied.

The Alphabet Race

A game students love to play with their cards is called the Alphabet Race. Have the class shake up their boxes so that all the letters are well mixed. Ask them to arrange the letters on their desk in alphabetical order. One time they will do it with uppercase letters and another time with the lowercase letters. The first student to finish the task correctly becomes the Alphabet King or Alphabet Queen for that day. Other students who finish within the allotted time may receive stickers or praise as an incentive. Those who are having difficulty competing may be praised for progress or be allowed to work at their own pace in a noncompetitive atmosphere.

Word Box

The word box is similar to the alphabet box except that it contains words instead of letters. The teacher starts by selecting high-frequency words such as a, look, but, can, do, good, etc., and reproducing them for the class on heavy paper or poster board. The teacher then passes out several words a day to each student for learning. Students are encouraged to add their own words to the box. Words that are encountered in reading or spelling, plus common nouns and verbs, may also be added. As the words mount up, students should gather enough words to begin to make sentences on their desks or on flash cards. Other uses for the word box include alphabetizing words, identifying letters or sounds in words, and identifying subject and verb, nouns, and so on.

Tongue Twisters

Teachers can help students identify sounds of the letters by associating each sound with a make-believe character, e.g., Billy Butler for b, Queen Quilla for q, and Talkative Ted for t. Children also enjoy memorizing and reciting strange sentences or tongue twisters. Both of these concepts come together in the following sample tongue twisters for consonants:

Billy Butler badly burned his bacon burgers.

Goofy guys go ga ga over girls.

Lonely Lucy Long laughs little lately.

Queen Quilla quit quilting quality quilts.

Seven silly sisters sang several silly songs.

Talkative Ted told ten terrible tales.

Ziggy the zebra "zigzags" in the zoo.

Letter Search

The teacher passes out a page from a newspaper or magazine and asks the students to find a certain letter on the page and circle the word in which they found it. Usually the teacher will limit the number of words to five or ten and then go on to a new letter. One variation is to ask students to start at the top of the page and find the letter a in a word and circle it. From there, they look for the letter b, circle it, then keep going in search of c, and so on, going as far through the alphabet as possible in the allotted time. Later on, students could search the newspapers for certain vowel digraphs or blends, silent letters, prefixes, two-letter words, six-letter words, etc.

Student ABC Books

As students are learning the sound of an individual letter, talk to them about how to make their own alphabet book.

Pass out a large sheet of heavyweight construction paper. Have each student print a rather large letter in both upper- and lowercase at the top of the page. Ask students to fill out the rest of the page with words that start with that letter or pictures of things whose name starts with that letter. As they encounter words in reading and spelling, they are encouraged to add these words to the page and draw a picture to represent each word. As students learn more letters, they may create pages for each new letter and begin to assemble the pages with some kind of binding. At times these pages can also be displayed on the walls of the classroom or in the school hallway.

Making an ABC book is an ongoing project that may last the whole year. As students continue to add new words and pictures to their books, they may add additional pages as the need arises. After all the letters are introduced, the teacher may take one page from each student and make a classroom ABC Book.

CONCLUSION

It is not an exaggeration to say that in the process of learning to read, the ability to identify letter names and sounds and to reproduce these letters holds the key to success or failure for most students. Research over the years heavily supports the importance of learning the alphabet as a first formal step in learning to read. For example, researchers have come to the following conclusions:

- Knowing the names of the letters is one of the best indicators of success in reading (Chall, 1967).
- The single best indicator of early reading achievement is accurate, rapid identification of upper- and lowercase letters of the alphabet. The second best indicator is phonemic awareness (Adams, 1998).
- The ability to name and recognize upper- and lowercase letters accounted for 25 to 36 percent of the variation in reading ability at the end of the first year, regardless of the method used to teach reading (Bond & Dykstra, 1967).
- "Until children can comfortably discriminate the shape of one letter from another, there is no point in teaching letter-sound pairings" (California Department of Education, 1996, p. 5).

Since learning the letters and sounds of the alphabet generally occurs before a child enters school or in kindergarten and first grade, it is natural to believe that once students get into later grades, they know how to write the letters. This is not always the case. Based on years of experience working with children who have reading and spelling problems, I suggest that parents and teachers of students who are struggling begin by finding out whether the students can identify and reproduce the letters in good form and order. In many of these cases, the alphabet is the starting point of the solution.

4

Teaching Consonants

The alphabet we use to write the English language is divided into two categories: consonants and vowels. Although almost every school-child is able to recite the alphabet and distinguish vowels from consonants, very few adults are able to explain the difference between the two. Vowels are defined as those sounds that pass freely and unrestricted through the mouth, and consonants are defined as those that are made by touching parts of the mouth or lips to each other.

DISTINGUISHING CONSONANTS AND VOWELS

The easiest way to explain the difference between consonants and vowels to students is to have them say the letters aloud so that they can actually feel what is happening in their mouths. A good teaching strategy is to ask students to say the letter names of the vowels several times aloud and in rapid succession: *A A A A A, E E E E E,* etc. They should be able to note and feel that, although the tongue moves to different positions for each vowel, it never obstructs the flow of air. Next, have students repeat the sounds of the consonant letters several times: *B B B B B, M M M M M, T T T T T,* etc. Students should be able to feel how the sound of each letter is restricted or obstructed by the tongue or lips. They will notice that air cannot escape without causing friction, which is heard differently for each letter. For teachers who wish to explore consonants in greater detail for themselves, Figure 4.1 lists the types of consonants.

Figure 4.1 Types of Consonants

Without going into great detail regarding the mechanics of how consonant sounds are reproduced, we can categorize them briefly as follows:

- Stopped consonants (plosives) that require a complete stoppage of breath: *b, d, g, k, p,* and *t*

- Open consonants (fricatives) that require only partial stoppage of breath: *l, m, n, r, w,* and *y*

- Spirants, or open consonants that produce friction in the oral passage: *f, j, s, v,* and *z*

- Aspirant, or breathed consonant, similar to a vowel: *h*

WHY TEACH CONSONANTS FIRST?

Although some reading authorities disagree about whether it is better to begin formalized reading instruction with vowels or consonants, most feel it is generally easier to start with the consonants. There are at least three good reasons to start with consonant sounds that appear at the beginning—in the initial position—of the word.

The first reason is that the majority of the words the student encounters in beginning reading programs begin with consonants (*dog, go, stop, run, mom,* etc.). In the *Developmental Word List* developed by Edward Fry (1995) for example, 156 of the 192 words listed begin with consonants. Another author points out that only eighteen of the most common five hundred nouns found in reading material for the early elementary grades begin with vowels (Blevins, 1998, p. 149).

Second, it makes good sense to start decoding skills at the beginning of the word, because this teaches students to focus on the first part of the word, where the pronunciation and phonemic analysis (if necessary) begins. It also facilitates and reinforces the left-to-right progression needed for successful reading. When the student is just beginning to identify sounds in words, it is better to start at the beginning, where the consonant sound is generally more dominant, than in the middle or at the end of the word, where it is less dominant (Daniels & Diack, 1956; Weaver, 1970, cited in Adams, 1998).

Third, it is generally better to start with consonants rather than vowels because consonants as a group are much more consistent in representing sounds (Adams, 1998). Whereas most consonants represent only one sound, vowels generally represent more than one sound (*go, do, some, woman,* etc.). Not only do all vowel letters represent more than one sound, but a single sound (such as the long /i/, for example) can also be represented by different vowel letters and spellings (*I, eye, high, my, dye, tie, ice, choir,* etc.). It is difficult enough for the beginning reader to learn how to read without starting students out on the rocky road of learning vowel sounds before they are ready. After students have mastered the sounds of the letters of the alphabet, have learned a few basic sight words, and have gained experience with identifying consonant sounds, then they can be exposed to the more complicated and less consistent vowel sounds with a greater assurance of success.

WHEN TO START TEACHING CONSONANTS

The exact time to start teaching structured or formalized phonics concepts and practices is, according to one reading authority, "an emotionally loaded question" (Fry, 1995, p. 14). Fry goes on to explain that the research is inconclusive, but he feels that some kind of structured awareness should begin in kindergarten in the form of readiness activities, such as playing with letters, coloring them, and listening to rhymes and poetry. He further suggests that regular reading lessons should begin in first grade and that a complete line of phonics should extend into the third grade, with some review, repetition, and, if necessary, remedial lessons later on.

Fry was talking about classroom teaching in that sense. Obviously, learning will be expedited if the child comes to school already equipped with some kind of readiness for learning sounds. Such activities as visiting the library, coloring letters in a coloring book, knowing the shapes of letters, singing the "Alphabet Song," being able to identify some words, and so on, lay a good foundation. Storytelling by parents, and especially reading aloud to children on a regular basis, will help prepare them for more formal instruction and give them a good incentive for learning to read.

INTRODUCING CONSONANTS

To assist in the learning of these sounds, it is recommended that early elementary teachers display a large alphabet chart at the front of the classroom or in a place where everyone can easily view it when instruction is given. The teacher should refer to the chart often, especially when the students are just beginning to learn the sounds. It is also recommended that each student have his or her own set of alphabet cards with pictures representing words that have each letter as the beginning sound. Occasionally, the teacher should ask the students to arrange their alphabet cards in proper alphabetical order. These cards can also be used to identify certain letters or sounds and for spelling short words. These kinds of manipulative activities are something children enjoy doing. Most important, they give the student early success experiences with the alphabet and greatly assist in learning the initial sounds of the letters.

When students are in the early stages of learning sounds, it is important to remember that teachers don't want to get them into the habit of isolating or overemphasizing the individual sounds of the letters. The student should not make a practice of trying to sound out all the phonemes in the word in such a manner that the pronunciation becomes abnormal, so that *bat* ends up sounding like *buh-ah-tuh.* It is important that the student learn that *bat* is a one-syllable word, not a three-syllable word. Some emphasis on each phoneme can be helpful at the beginning stages of learning sounds, but overemphasis and unnatural distortion can soon become a stumbling block for learners.

Obviously, many different ways of getting started exist. It's impossible to go into detail about all the techniques teachers have used over the years to introduce consonant sounds. In cases where a teacher is unsure of how to begin, several methods can be chosen to introduce initial consonant sounds to the class. One approach is to write one of the consonants in both upper- and lowercase on the board and ask the students to identify it. Next, ask for volunteers to name words that begin with that particular consonant and list them on the board (*B, b: boy, box, baseball, Ben, baby*). When students run out of ideas, ask them to put the words in a sentence, spell them, and then write them down on paper to save for future reference.

Another popular activity is to have the children rummage through old magazines and newspapers to find pictures of objects with names that begin with the letter or letters they are learning. Have the children cut out the pictures and glue them on a sheet of paper that contains that letter. They can make their own personal letter scrapbook or contribute their page for a classroom alphabet book, or both. Another version of the same idea is to have students draw pictures of objects that start with a certain letter (*b: butterfly; c: cat; d: dog,* etc.), cut out the pictures, and paste them on a large sheet of poster board. This poster board can then be placed on the chalkboard ledge for easy viewing and reference. The number of poster-board drawings will increase as more and more letters are learned. They can be easily stored for future reference and review.

Perhaps the best way to get ideas about how to introduce and reinforce consonants (or any other skill, for that matter) is to ask successful teachers what methods they find effective. Good, experienced classroom teachers know what works and what doesn't, and are often the best resources.

Should Students Memorize Rules?

Before explaining the rules for consonant sounds, it is important to say a few words about rules in general. The majority of the so-called rules that govern the structure of the English language, especially those related to the pronunciation and spelling of English, are generally so vague and confusing that memorizing them is not especially helpful to students (Clymer, 1963). For example, the " *i* before *e*, except after *c*, or when sounding as *a*, as in *neighbor* and *weigh*" rule is correct about two-thirds of the time. So those who follow that rule are wrong one-third of the time. Another rule stating that the *e* at the end of a word makes the vowel before it long is wrong about 40 percent of the time. Still another rule says that when two vowels come together in a word, "the first does the talking (is long) and the second does the walking (is silent). " Yet when students later come across a common word such as *said, heart, head, great, friend,* etc. and then apply that rule when reading aloud, the same teacher scolds them for being wrong.

On the other hand, it is important to remember that just as some rules or generalizations have too many exceptions to be useful, and rote memorization of some rules can be a waste of time and effort, most rules are, or can be, helpful. If students aren't sure if a word is spelled *ie* or *ei*, knowing the rule helps them make decisions that are more often correct than incorrect. Rules for dividing words into syllables, capitalization, punctuation, pronunciation, for forming plurals, etc. can be extremely helpful—if not essential—for developing reading, spelling, and writing skills. The big thing is not to throw out the baby with the bathwater.

When it comes to learning rules, teachers can present them in several ways that do not cause as much confusion or as many problems. First, stop calling them rules and start referring to them as generalizations or tendencies. Next, present enough examples of certain types of words so that students will note or discover how these generalizations work in the given situations. This means students must have opportunities to investigate words in order to discover relationships and tendencies—to find out which generalizations are reliable and which are not.

An excellent way to get students to internalize these tendencies is to give them plenty of practice with phonograms (Wylie & Durrell, 1970). If students see and have enough experience with words that have the same ending (*take, bake, cake,* etc.), they will learn (without being taught) that the *e* at the end in these examples makes the *a* before it long. When students read a list of one-syllable words that end in *y* (*try, my, sky, buy,* etc.) they will learn, without memorizing a rule, that the *y* at the end of a one-syllable word generally has the long /i/ sound. Working with phonograms in this manner gives students a chance to internalize the generalization so that they apply that knowledge automatically when situations require it. In other words, students will be using a generalization without knowing it is a generalization. Through experience with words and the variations of spelling, students will discover over a period of time what tendencies they can depend on and which ones they should be cautious about. However the teacher manages it, students must become more aware of word tendencies, rather than be presented with a list of "rules."

Having said that, one should not conclude that elementary teachers can just go ahead and ignore the rules. Knowledge of the generalizations and tendencies is important for the teacher because they give an idea of what concepts have meaning and relevance—what should be taught and what should not be taught and why. One reading authority points out that rules, or generalizations, give particular attention to an aspect of spelling under study and, as such, have value (Adams, 1998). Rules can also be used to strengthen the association that binds spelling combinations together and can be helpful for the learner in organizing, noticing, and reinforcing relationships (Adams, 1998).

TEACHING CONSONANTS IN THE INITIAL POSITION

Assuming the students have learned a few sight words and can identify most of the letters of the alphabet, they are now ready for the next logical step: learning the consonant sounds at the beginning of the word.

The most widespread technique for teaching initial consonants is to begin with those that can be pronounced in isolation with the least distortion (Adams, 1998). The consonants that represent one sound—*b, d, f, h, k, 1, m, n, p, r, t, v, w, y* (in the initial position), and *z*—should be taught first. These consonants can flourish both in isolation and in words in which they occur (Adams, 1998). Later on, when children have had some successful experiences identifying more consistent consonants, they will be able to work with consonants (*c, s, g*) that have two sounds and are less consistent.

It should be noted that *y* is always a consonant when it is found at the beginning of the word (*yes, year, your,* etc.) and is a vowel when found in the middle or at the end of a word (*by, nicely,* etc.). The letter *x* is excluded from the consonant list above because very few words, almost all of which are hyphenated, begin with that letter (*x-ray, X-rated, X-mas,* etc.). The letter *x* is redundant to the extent that, when it starts a word it almost always represents the /z/ sound (*xylophone, xenophobic, xebec,* etc.).

It is a good idea to avoid teaching letters in the same session that can be confused with each other in form or sound. Words that begin with letters similar in form—such as *d* and *b, m* and *n,* or *g* and *q*—are best presented in separate lessons so as not to confuse students. By the same token, it is not a good idea to teach letters that have similar sounds in the same lesson, for example, *c* and *s* or *g* and *j.* Later, when students have had more experience and practice with initial sounds, these letters may be presented together and the differences pointed out.

Generalizations for Sounds of Initial Consonants

One of the handy features of initial consonants is that they are quite consistent in the sounds they represent. Most of the initial consonants consistently represent only one sound. Even the few letters that have more than one sound (*c: cat, cell* and *g: gem, go*) follow patterns that are consistent and can be easily understood. Generalizations for initial consonants need not be memorized. The general knowledge of this consistency, however, can be helpful for learning new words.

- When the consonants *b, d, f, j, k, 1, m, n, p, r, t, v, w, y,* and *z* appear at the beginning of a word, they generally represent one sound.
- When the consonant *c* is followed by *a, o,* or *u,* it has the /k/ sound (*corn, cat, curl*). When *c* is followed by *e, i,* or *y,* it has the sound of /s/ (*city, cent, cycle*).
- When the consonant *g* is followed by *e, i,* or *y,* it may have the sound of /j/ (*gem, giant, gym*). Most of the time *g* has the sound of /g/ (*good, gum, get*).
- The consonant *q* has the sound of /kw/ (*queen, quit, quack*).
- The letter *q* never appears by itself at the beginning of a word. It is always followed by the letter *u* (*queen, question, quiet*).
- When the consonant *s* appears at the beginning of a word, it generally has the /s/ sound (*sun, soon, sat*). Occasionally, the *s* may have the

sound of /sh/ or /zh/ (*sugar, treasure*). The /s/ sound may also be represented at the beginning of a word by the consonant *c* when the *c* is followed by an *e, i,* or *y* (*city, cent, cycle*). At the end of a word the s may represent the /z/ sound (*his, runs*).

- The consonant *x* generally has the sound of /z/ at the beginning of a word (*xylem, Xerox*). A few hyphenated words (*x-ray, X-rated*) begin with *x*.

Figure 4.2 contains lists of words grouped according to their initial letter. The groups are presented in alphabetical order not because this is a recommended way to teach them, but rather to make them easier for the reader to follow and understand. For the most part, these are words that students in kindergarten and first grade have heard or seen in print materials used at home or in school. They are generally one-syllable words and can be learned without much difficulty by the majority of the students in the early grades. A teacher can either start with the words below or begin by having the students make up the list. It must be emphasized that the purpose of this list, and all the others in this book, is to give examples that may or may not be used according to teaching needs. They are not intended to be prescriptive.

Figure 4.2   Initial Consonants

b	c (k)	c (s)	d	f	g
book	cat	cell	day	fish	game
boy	car	cite	did	fast	got
base	came	city	dike	fog	gave
been	cup	center	dish	fade	gang
ball	cook	cellar	do	fang	goat
big	call	circle	dump	fight	gone
box	come	cider	done	fit	get
bat	coat	circus	dare	fix	give
bet	corn	central	disk	form	gum
bit	cow	cycle	dew	fun	gap
but	cap	cent	ding	food	gate
bench	cut		does	fox	

(Continued)

(Continued)

g (j)	h	j	k	l	m
gee	hat	jet	keep	love	me
gem	her	jump	kick	look	more
gym	hit	just	kid	like	must
giant	his	jam	key	live	much
germ	hurt	job	kin	let	most
gentle	hot	join	kiss	list	men
ginger	hen	jar	king	loot	mind
gene	hint	joy	kink	lock	mint
genus	hand	jade	keen	luck	miss
George	has	jest	kite	line	milk
gibe	ham	jeep	kit	lurk	mouse
gerbil	home	jail	kind	lake	might

n	p	q(qu)	r	s	t
no	pan	quick	run	sad	to
not	pen	queen	red	son	tight
nut	pin	quest	row	so	test
nice	pal	quack	rug	sing	tent
nor	post	quite	road	sang	tube
neck	put	quit	roar	sat	toes
night	pain	quiz	read	sunk	ten
neat	pair	quote	ride	sum	tip
noon	patch	quart	rip	sock	toss
nun	park	quartz	room	sink	two
nest	pig		ring	sand	time
name	paint		rim	sung	top

v	w	y	z		
van	we	you	zip		
voice	went	yet	zing		
vane	want	young	zoo		
vote	were	yam	zoom		
vest	was	your	zinc		
vow	war	yeast	zeal		
vent	will	yell	zest		
verse	wall	year	zone		
vine	wow	yolk	zap		
vain	walk	yawn			
vase	well	yes			
	wolf				

Musical Consonants

One music activity that fits in nicely with learning initial consonants is to have students sing familiar songs, but substitute sounds for words. The "Happy Birthday" song, "Twinkle, Twinkle, Little Star," and "I've Been Working on the Railroad," for example, can be sung by repeating a sound over and over again using the rhythm and tune of the song (*bah, bah, bah; zee, zee, zee; no, no, no,* etc.). Or a song such as "Old MacDonald" can be adapted and the letters changed as needed:

Old MacDonald had a farm

M, I, M, I, O.

And on that farm he had an M

M, I, M, I, O.

With an M right here,

And an M right there,

(and so on)

TEACHING PHONOGRAMS OR COMMON ENDINGS

Once the students have learned and have had plenty of practice with the initial consonant sounds, they are ready to go on to the second stage of phonics instruction—learning about phonograms, or word families (Burns, 2006). Fry (1993) describes a phonogram as follows: "A phonogram is usually a vowel sound plus a consonant sound, but it is often less than a word—it needs an initial consonant or blend to make it a word." Words that rhyme contain the same phonograms (e. g., *king, sing, thing; at, fat, cat*).

If students have learned the word *run* and learned the initial sounds of most consonants, they ought to be able to use that knowledge to figure out, or sound out, more words with similar sounds, such as *fun, nun,* and *pun.* If children know the word *at* they should find it easier to read and spell words in the same family (*fat, hat, rat, mat,* etc.). If children can recognize and pronounce the word *sing,* then *king, ring, wing,* and even *zing* should come quite naturally.

One of the nice features about teaching and learning phonograms is that although vowels and vowel digraphs in words are generally difficult to decode for young children, sounds in phonograms are relatively easy to read (Clymer, 1963). Wylie and Durrell (1970) reinforce this conclusion. They reported that in a list of 286 rimes (word endings) that appear in primary texts, the vowels of 272 (95 percent) are pronounced the same way in every word in which they are found. They further point out that nearly five hundred primary grade words can be derived from just thirty-seven rimes (-ack, -ail, -ain, -ake, -ale, -ame, -an, -ank, -ap, -ash, -at, -ate, -aw, -ay, -eat, -ell, -est, -ice, -ick, -ide, -ight, -ill, -in, -ine, -ing, -ink, -ip, -ir, -ock, -oke, -op, -or, -ore, -uck, -ug, -ump, -unk).

Phonograms are also a great aid in teaching vowel sounds. Because vowel sounds are inconsistent—a single vowel can represent different sounds and, inversely, a single sound may be represented by different vowels—they are generally difficult to teach and categorize. Using phonograms, however, vowels can be put into groups according to similar spelling patterns and, as we know that they all rhyme, the vowels will be pronounced the same. This goes for long vowels and short vowels and for vowel digraphs and silent vowels.

One of the more important reasons for learning phonograms is to give the student a valuable tool for figuring out polysyllabic words. For example, the ending *at* as in *-bat, -fat,* and *-mat* is also a syllable in longer words—*attic, mathematics, habitat,* etc. Tens of thousands of polysyllabic words in English contain letter combinations such as *-ing, -ent, -ell,* and *-or,* at the beginning, the middle, or the end. Being able to recognize these sounds in words will be extremely valuable later in life when the student becomes more exposed to words that are not seen very often or that are part of the vocabulary of an unfamiliar science or vocation. Without the ability to see and recognize familiar sounds in longer or unfamiliar words, even adults would be more likely to stumble over the pronunciation and spelling of words and names.

Although using word families is a very popular method of teaching sounds in today's classrooms, the method has been around for centuries

(Smith, 1986). In colonial days, Noah Webster's old "blue-backed speller" (one of the best-selling textbooks of all times) used phonograms to teach spelling, which in turn was used to teach reading. Phonograms can be as valuable a means of learning reading and spelling today as they were back then. (See Figures 4.3 and 4. 4 for lists of common phonograms.)

One of the more popular ways of introducing phonograms is to have students participate in compiling the list rather than just reproducing it and then passing it out to be learned. It's a simple procedure:

1. Write a known word on the board that contains one of the phonograms—*hat,* for example.

2. Have students pronounce the word, spell the word, and use it in a sentence. They should then write the word on a sheet of paper.

3. Erase the original initial consonant and substitute another consonant—*b,* for example. Write the new word on the board and ask the students to say the word.

4. Ask for another word that rhymes with *hat* and *bat,* and write it on the board. Have students use the word in a sentence and add it to their lists.

5. Repeat the steps until students cannot add any new words. If the list is small, the teacher might suggest a word or two.

6. Have students save this list for spelling, writing, and review purposes.

There is absolutely nothing wrong with the teacher's making a list of rhyming words for students and distributing it for review, rote reading, creative writing, or other kinds of activities.

Hink Pinks

A fun writing activity that coordinates well with writing and spelling is to have students make up "hink pinks," or pairs of rhyming words. Hink pinks help students discover the spelling pattern of words in the same family. If students enjoy making a collection of their favorite hink pinks, this could be an ongoing project. Here are a few the teacher might use to get the children started: glum chum, low blow, fish dish, fat cat, ten men, blew stew, loose goose. Who can make the most? Who has the funniest one? Can anyone think of "hinky pinkies," or two-syllable rhyming words, such as double trouble? This project can also be extended to art classes, where a student might want to draw a picture of a fat cat, loose goose, wet pet, etc.

Figure 4.3   Sixty Most Common Phonograms

Word endings that are found in twelve or more words

ab	ame	ay	ent	ip	out
ack	amp	eak	est	it	ow (o)
ad	an	ear	ick	ock	ow (ou)
ag	ane	eat	ide	od	uck
ail	ank	ed	ig	og	ug
ain	are	eed	ight	one	um
ake	ap	eep	ill	ook	ump
ale	ash	ell	in	op	unk
all	at	en	ine	ore	ut
am	ave	end	ing	ot	y (i)

Figure 4.4   Sixty More Phonograms

Word endings that appear in fewer than twelve words

awl	eek	ile	oll	ud
awn	eel	ilt	ool	udge
axe	een	ime	oon	ue
each	eer	ipe	oop	uff
ead	eet	ive	orn	ull
eal	ench	oat	ose	un
eam	ice	ob	oss	unt
ean	id	oft	ouch	ush
eck	ies	oke	ound	ut
ee	ike	old	own	ute

Verse Completion

Another suggestion that works very well with younger children in kindergarten and first grade is to read to them from a book of verse. Pause before the rhyme and then let students supply the missing word. After a verse has been read, encourage the class to recite the verse together with the teacher in a singsong manner. Allow the students to clap their hands to denote the rhythm. See if they can even make up their own little song around the verse.

TEACHING ENDING CONSONANT SOUNDS

Consonant sounds that appear at the end of a word may be taught in somewhat the same manner as initial consonant sounds. Start with a word the class knows. The students listen to the final consonant sound and then give examples of other words that have that same final sound.

The examples in Figure 4.5, like most of the words in the other lists in this book, are one-syllable words and are well within the speaking and listening vocabularies of children in first and second grades. Unlike the listings for phonograms, these words will not be as easy to spell or write because they might contain vowel spellings that are not familiar. This is one of the reasons ending consonants should be taught after students have had some experience with initial consonants and phonograms. Many of the phonograms listed in Figures 4.3 and 4.4 are contained in the list in Figure 4.5.

Figure 4.5   Ending Consonant Sounds

/b/	/d/	/f/	/g/	/k/	/l/	/m/
cob	red	if	big	work	fail	ham
lab	kid	wolf	rug	kick	call	time
job	wed	wife	fig	make	ill	room
tub	mud	safe	lug	duck	sell	gum
bib	good	off	wig	tock	tall	gem
cab	read	leaf	dog	desk	cool	bum
tab	bid	turf	bag	luck	fool	come
mob	bold	puff	keg	lake	mill	him
rib	head	half	sag	cook	mile	home

(Continued)

(Continued)

web	loud	life	lag	mark	girl	dumb
tube	did	roof	mug	take	heel	same
bob	bad	golf	bug	dock	tool	harm

/n/	/p/	/r/	/s/	/t/	/v/	/z/
an	pip	dear	gas	feet	save	is
gone	lap	hair	boats	hot	give	ease
fin	lip	tar	house	kit	leave	ties
corn	soap	hear	miss	get	dove	was
pun	jeep	her	bliss	hat	love	size
seen	pup	fair	dress	meat	gave	fuzz
pine	hope	jar	worse	coat	drive	quiz
tan	map	fur	yes	lot	live	he's
done	whip	bear	mess	mat	dive	tease
soon	zap	jeer	nurse	foot	wave	rise
win	ship	sure	lass	boat	move	does
fun	rope	for	purse	cut	hive	his

Word Detective

Students generally have more problems with the sounds of ending consonants than they do with those at the beginning of the word. An activity that really aids in identifying endings is to play word detective. Ask the class to open their reading book to a page that has a lot of print. Ask them to make a list of the words they find on that page (or in that story) that end in the letters you want them to identify. Which ending is found most often? A variation of this activity is to give students an assignment (or homework) asking them to find five words that end with *k* in the daily newspaper, ten words that end with *s*, etc. This is a good way to get parents involved.

TEACHING INITIAL CONSONANT BLENDS AND DIGRAPHS

Consonant blends are formed when two consonants come together to form a blending or gliding sound that slightly affects the separate sound of each letter—the /gr/ sound as in *grass*, the /bl/ sound as in *black*, and the /sp/ sound as in *spell*, for example.

Consonant digraphs are formed when two consonants come together to form a separate sound unlike those of either letter—the /ch/ sound as in *child*, the /wh/ sound as in *when*, and the /th/ sound as in *thin*, for example. Figure 4.6 contains examples of words with initial blend sounds.

Figure 4.6   Initial Blend Sounds

br	cr	dr	fr	gr	pr	tr
brace	crow	draw	from	grow	print	trade
brush	crest	dress	frank	greet	prank	tray
brim	crate	drew	friend	grin	prince	treat
brake	crisp	dream	frog	gripe	pray	trace
bring	crimp	drop	free	green	prize	trip
brought	cry	drip	fresh	gray	proof	truck
bright	cram	drum	fruit	grew	prop	train
brother	crack	drill	fright	grape	prong	track
brain	crisp	drove	frost	grit	price	trash
bridge	cream	drink	fry	gruff	pry	try
brook	crude	drank	front	group	press	true
brag	crook	drive	frame	grace	pride	trap

bl	cl	f	gl	pl	sl	tw
black	click	flame	glad	play	slow	twenty
bliss	class	fling	glow	plow	slap	twist

(Continued)

(Continued)

blend	cling	flop	glide	plate	slant	twin
blow	close	fly	glen	place	slug	twelve
bless	clam	flake	glance	plunge	slim	twine
blot	cloud	flip	glue	plane	slate	twang
bleach	climb	flap	gloom	plug	slide	tweak
blame	clear	fled	glee	plight	slice	twig
blare	clock	flight	glitch	plot	slash	tweeze
blaze	clip	flesh	gloat	plump	slip	tweet
blast	clog	flow	glut	plain	sleep	twice
blue	clove	flew	glib	plank	slick	tweed

sc	sk	sm	sn	sp	st	sw
scold	skip	small	snip	spill	star	swing
score	sky	smell	snort	spell	start	sway
scant	skill	smile	snap	spoil	steer	swell
scan	skate	smart	snow	spoon	stair	swipe
scar	skull	smug	snug	sponge	stay	sweet
scoff	skit	smog	snare	speak	state	swear
scare	skin	smooth	snail	spin	stale	swam
scab	ski	smack	snub	spit	stick	swim
scarf	skid	smoke	sniff	sped	stall	swat
scamp	skirt	smear	snake	spine	stash	swift
	skunk		snoop	speed	stage	swoop
	skim		snore	spot		swish

scr	squ	str	thr	spr	spl	shr
scrub	square	straw	three	spring	splash	shrill
scream	squad	stray	through	sprain	splice	shrink
screw	squint	stream	thrown	sprite	spleen	shrug
scrimp	squeak	strong	throng	spry	splint	shrank
script	squash	straight	throne	spray	splat	shrunk
scrap	squirt	string	throat	spread	splurge	shrine
scruff	squeal	strip	threw	sprung	splotch	shriek
scribe	squeeze	strange	thrill	spruce	split	shred
screen	squawk	strike	throb	sprout		shrub
scratch	squid	stripe	thrive	sprig		shrewd
scroll		street	throw	sprawl		
		strap				

Once students learn the twenty-six letters of the alphabet and begin to associate sounds with those letters, they soon discover that consonants—and especially vowels—can represent more than one sound. They also learn that when certain letters are side by side they can form a distinct sound different from that associated with either letter. In the process of learning sounds and words, students discover that there are at least twenty-five different pronunciations for consonants, and that there are at least thirty-three more ways these consonants can blend together to form new sounds. This adds up to a total of at least fifty-eight different ways consonants (by themselves or in conjunction with another consonant or consonants) can represent sounds. Is it any wonder, then, that it takes some students so long to learn how to read and that practice and repetition are so necessary?

One of the most convenient features about blends and consonant digraphs is that they consistently represent only one sound. Once students learn certain blend sounds, they can depend on that consistency. For this reason, blends and consonant digraphs are easily learned by most students and are rarely the source of spelling mistakes.

Having previous experience of working with consonant sounds and phonograms makes it easier for students to move on to the next step of learning blends and digraphs. If they are able to read the words *lack* and *back,* for example, and if they can pronounce the phonogram *-ack,* it should be fairly easy to put this information together and learn the new word *black.* The /bl/ never changes its sound, so students can go on to forming other *bl* words with common phonograms, such as *blow, bliss, blend, blare, blame,* etc.

It must be pointed out that the example of how a student can use knowledge of consonant sounds to learn blend sounds is more theoretical than practical. It is presented as an example of logical sequencing in order to demonstrate how learning one skill can assist in learning another. It works this way, however, only when students are at a particular stage of learning. It is a fact that some students already know many blend sounds before they know what the initial consonants are or even know all the letters of the alphabet. It is important to remember that many students will never need explicit instruction in the particular skills mentioned in this chapter and other sections of the book, because they have already internalized them in their own way and do not need additional practice. For a few students, all that's needed is a good book that interests them, and all the problems that haunt other students are irrelevant. In other words, the examples presented here should be learned by the teacher so that the information can be used when and in whatever order it is needed. It is not intended for every student in every situation.

Blend Twisters

A good way to help students become more aware of the sounds of initial blends and digraphs, and to give them more practice with these sounds, is to have them write "blend twisters," or sentences that have words that begin with the same blend sound. Although it is generally better to have students come up with their own twisters, the following ones may serve to get them started or as a reminder of how these sounds behave. For example:

Snappy snails sniff snoring snakes.

Skinny skeletons ski skillfully skyward.

Green growing grass gradually grows gray.

Shifty sharks shatter shiny ships.

Friendly Freddie frees Frank from frisky frogs.

TEACHING SILENT CONSONANTS

One of the most debilitating factors for teaching letter-sound relationships is the fact that as many as one-sixth of all our words have silent letters in

Figure 4.7 Silent Consonants

double	m(b)	(c)k	i(gh)	(k)n	(t)en	(w)r
happy	bomb	rock	fight	knock	often	wrap
letter	climb	tick	eight	knew	listen	write
dinner	comb	tock	weight	know	hasten	wrote
supper	lamb	tack	might	knee	soften	wrong
jell	dumb	duck	right	kneel	fasten	wreak
zipper	tomb	block	straight	knife	brighten	wren
summer	thumb	deck	flight	knit	glisten	wrist
mitten	numb	black	light	knob	moisten	wreck
ladder	limb	lock	night	knob		wreath
collect	crumb	pick	high	knack		

them. The most frequent occurrences of silent letters are in vowel sounds. The silent *e* at the end of a word that sometimes causes the vowel before it to become long (*rope, game,* etc.) and vowel digraphs where one of the vowels is silent (*dead, build,* etc.) are the two primary culprits.

The most frequent occurrence of silent consonants is the doubling of consonants that often appears in the middle of words (*letter, message, dinner,* etc.). Whereas these double consonants pose no problems in reading (*letter* and *leter* are generally both pronounced alike), double letters do present a major problem in spelling. The omission of one of the doubled letters (*beter, begining, sorow,* etc.) is incorrect, as is the doubling of other letters that should not be doubled (*trainning, bussiness, writting, doubble,* etc.). It's not possible to tell just from the pronunciation when those double consonants should be used.

One of the positive features of silent consonants is that most of them are very predictable and can be taught as generalizations. Again, it is not recommended that students memorize these generalizations. It is recommended, however, that students be given opportunities to work with words that contain the silent letters to become familiar with the word patterns. With enough exposure and practice students should have little trouble with silent letters.

Figure 4.7 is a list of silent consonants and common words that contain them.

Generalizations Concerning Silent Consonants

- When a word contains a double consonant in the middle (*butter, summer, sudden,* etc.) it is sounded as a single consonant.

- When a word ends in *mb,* the *b* is generally silent (*lamb, climb, dumb,* etc.).
- When a word ends in *ck,* the *c* is generally silent (*kick, duck, back,* etc.).
- When a word begins with *wr,* the *w* is generally silent (*wren, wrist, wrong,* etc.).
- When a word begins with *kn,* the *k* is generally silent (*know, knife, knit,* etc.).
- When the letters *gh* are preceded by an *i,* the *gh* is generally silent (*right, night, brighten,* etc.).
- There are no good generalizations for other silent consonants such as the silent *l* (*half, folks,* etc.) , the silent *g* (*sign, gnash, reign,* etc.), and the silent *h* (*hour, ghost, honor,* etc.). (Heilman, 1966)

Silent Letter Detective

An entertaining activity for making students more aware of the silent letters in words and their frequency in print is to have them play word detective from time to time to find out how many silent letters occur in a particular story or article. Have students write out the words they find and then categorize them according to similarities of spelling. Another way to cause some excitement about silent letters is to designate a space on the blackboard for words that contain them. Whenever students encounter a word with a silent letter that day, allow them to go to the board and write it in the space provided. This list could include not only silent consonants but silent vowels and vowel digraphs as well. This activity is not recommended as daily practice. Every once in a while should be sufficient to serve the purpose.

CONCLUSION

In this chapter, I have presented a great deal of material about teaching consonants along with information about rules and plenty of examples. The material is introduced in ascending order—from easier concepts to more complicated ones—to show a logical or natural flow for these skills. The order in which the concepts are presented reflects how most children would go about learning them.

Formalized phonics instruction first begins with teaching students individual letters and showing them how to blend them together to make words (Stahl et al., 1998). This formal process usually takes place in first grade, although the foundation is laid in kindergarten and preschool activities, especially those involving books. The second step is to assist the students not only in learning how to analyze the sounds of letters, but also in putting them together to make words. This process can be made most effective by exposing students to word families (phonograms), which have similar sounds and sound spellings that aid students in learning new words. As one authority put it, "Phonograms provide a useful bridge to the level of phonemic and phonological awareness upon which skilled reading depends" (Adams, 1998, p. 327).

As students begin to develop a greater awareness of sounds and spelling patterns and become able to recognize some high-frequency words that do not conform to normal or regular patterns (*do, love, come, said,* etc.), they become better prepared to tackle more advanced skills involving digraphs and blends. They become more capable of decoding more complicated spelling patterns. This usually occurs in second or third grade. Other skills involving word structure, syllabication, affixes, and word analysis are put off to the later grades.

When planning lessons to teach consonants and other phonics topics, it is important to remember that phonics instruction should generally be of short duration. There ought to be a specific reason for using it. It should be integrated into as many language-arts projects as possible. And phonics activities need not be boring. With a little thought and planning, they can become interesting, and maybe even fun!

5

Teaching
Vowel Sounds

For many teachers, having to teach vowel sounds is not only one of the least enjoyable aspects of teaching reading, it is also one of the most difficult. Students find it equally frustrating, and they generally make far more errors in reading the vowels in words than the consonants (Adams, 1998). The first problem the teacher faces is trying to determine just how many vowel sounds there are in the first place. While it is generally believed that English has only five real vowels—*a, e, i, o, u,* and sometimes a sixth, *y*—some linguists postulate that other letters such as *w, l,* and *r* can, at times, also be considered vowels or semivowels.

SOUNDS AND SPELLINGS OF VOWELS

While the discussion about the exact number of vowels is worthy of note, this number doesn't really have much importance when it comes to teaching reading. It's not the number of vowel letters, or graphemes, that's important; it's the number of vowel sounds, or phonemes. English may have five, six, or seven vowel graphemes, depending upon what definition is used to define a vowel, but it also has approximately twenty to twenty-two different vowel phonemes, which can be spelled or represented in hundreds of different ways (Pitman & St. John, 1969).

Whereas consonants, for the most part, are fairly consistent in sound and spelling and can be taught in a straightforward manner, vowels come in a wide variety of both sounds and spellings. Not only would it be virtually impossible to teach and learn all the various combinations of spellings, but to even attempt this task would also be seriously discouraging for students.

64

Figure 5.1 is a listing of vowel sounds and the more common spellings of these sounds. It must be noted that because of dialectical differences, many words such as *because, been, alms,* and *half,* which have more than one acceptable pronunciation, may very well fit into several categories. It is also difficult to compare vowel sounds when the only evidence is the written material. The listing below serves the purpose of pointing out to teachers the many spellings of each phoneme so that they may be taught when appropriate. The listing also demonstrates in a graphic manner the difficult problem vowels pose for children as they learn to read.

Figure 5.1

Vowel Phonemes and Graphemes

Phoneme	Graphemes	Examples
/ă/ (cat)	a, ai, al, au	cat, plait, calf, laugh
/ā/ (make)	a, a–e, ay, ai, aigh e, ea, ee, ei, eigh, ey	able, take, play, train, straight forte, great, melee, eight, they
/âr/ (care)	are, ai, ay, e, ea	care, fair, prayer, there, wear
/ä/ (father)	a, ah, al, e, ea	father, shah, palm, sergeant, hearth
/ĕ/ (bet)	e, a, ai, ay, e, ea, eo ie, u	end, many, said, says, set, head, leopard friend, bury
/ē/ tree	e, ea, ee, ei	me, leap, meet, receive
/ĭ/ (in)	i, y, a, ee, ia, ie, o, u, ui	pill, hymn, village, been carriage, sieve, women, busy, guilty
/ī/ (eye)	i–e, y, ai, ay, ei, uy, y, ye	mine, my, aisle, aye, height, buy, sky, rye
/îr/ (fear)	e, ea, ee, ei, ie	here, tear, beer, weird, pier
/ŏ/ (not)	o, a, ho, ou	hot, what, honest, trough
/ō/ (no)	o, o–e, eau, eo, ew oa, oe, oh, oo, ou, ough, ow, owe	no, vote, bureau, yeoman, sew, board, foe, oh, brooch, shoulder though, low, owe
/ô/ (fall)	a, al, ah, au, aw, ou	all, talk, Utah, daughter, paw, trough
/oi/ (oil)	oi, oy	noise, toy
/ou/ (mouse)	ou, ow, ough	house, now, bough

(Continued)

(Continued)

/oo/ (cook)	oo, u, o, oul	look, full, woman, could
/oo/ (toot)	oo, u–e, eu, ew o, eo, ou, ough, eu, ui	boot, rule, rheumatic, drew move, canoe, croup, through, blue, fruit
/ŭ / (cut)	u, o, oe, ou	but, some, does, trouble
/yoo/ (use)	u, u–e, eau, eu, ew ieu, iew, ue, you	use, yule, beauty, feud, few adieu, view, cue, you
/ûr/ (fern)	er, ir, or, ur, our	stern, first, work, burn, journey

Vowels are like chameleons—just as chameleons change their colors according to their environment, vowels change sounds according to the surrounding letters. For example, the most frequently used letter in English is *e*. And look at all the phonemic problems that accompany it! In most cases, a single *e* indicates the short /e/ sound, as in *spent, end, vowel,* etc. When it combines with another vowel, however, it can help change an accompanying vowel into a long vowel and help represent the sound of five long vowels: /a/–*weigh*; /e/–*feet*; /i/–*pie*; /o/–*doe*; /u/–*true*. When an *e* appears at the end of the word, it is generally silent and often makes the vowel before it long (*home, dive, save,* etc.). Then again, it sometimes doesn't make the vowel before it long (*love, come, gone,* etc.). The short /e/ can be represented in at least ten different ways; the long /e/ can be represented in fourteen ways. The other vowel sounds have almost the same kind of diversity problems, with the long /o/, which can be spelled or written in at least twenty-five different ways, leading the way (Pitman & St. John, 1969).

The good news is that, when examined, the vowel confusion problems become ever less confusing. For example, let's take a closer look at the spelling patterns of the five hundred words of the American Heritage Word List that most often occur in printed material in elementary grades. Thirty-five words in the list contain the long /a/ sound and six different spelling patterns. At first glance this would seem to pose a big problem for someone who wanted to use the sounding-out method. With further investigation, however, it soon becomes apparent that twenty-six of the thirty-four words have one of two consistent patterns that can be easily learned. Two other words have a consistent vowel digraph (a-) to indicate pronunciation.

Three words slightly misdirect pronunciation, and only two words, *they* and *great,* misdirect the vowel sound. These two words could easily be learned as sight words. Figure 5.2 breaks down the spellings of some words taken from the American Heritage list that have the long /a/ sound. These alternative patterns may, and often do, cause spelling problems when one tries to determine which one to use, but they do not generally cause confusion in reading; students automatically pronounce the words correctly because of how they are used in a sentence. No student would say, for

Figure 5.2

Spellings for the Long /a/ Sound

a–e	-ay	-ai-	-ea-	-a-	-ey
make	way	rain	great	table	they
made	day	tail		baby	
same	may			paper	
take	say				
page	away				
gave	always				
change	play				
place	days				
face	ways				
names	today				
space	stay				
game	maybe				
came					
makes					
name					
places					

example, "Mother held the *bah-by* in her arms," thinking the /a/ sound is short; nor would he or she read "Dad read the *pah-per*." Even though normally a single a might tend toward the /ah/ sound, the whole environment of the word leads the reader to the correct pronunciation. The letters in a word may not always lead to the exact pronunciation, but they generally take us close enough, so that the word's pronunciation is easily surmised from the context in which it is used. Like much else in life, our sound spellings may not be perfect, but they are good enough to be useful.

TEACHING VOWEL SOUNDS

Fortunately, students don't have to deal with every permutation of every vowel all at once, or even at all, in the early stages of reading. As with consonants, if vowels are presented correctly, students soon discover that learning just one word or sound can serve as a building block in learning other words and sounds. By noting similarities and differences in sounds and words and applying what they learn to new situations, students quickly discover that as one bit of knowledge leads to another, so one success leads to another, so that what they once thought was a difficult task becomes easier and easier with greater exposure and experience. As students practice these sounds, they will develop automatic word recognition so that they can concentrate more fully on the meaning of the text (Ehri, 1995).

It's important at this point to remind the teacher that phonics only goes so far, and that other approaches and ideas can also help students. Phonics is not the only means of teaching reading, nor is it the whole package. Far from it. It is precisely because students cannot depend entirely on symbol-sound relationships that they need to learn to use context, structure, and the meaning of other words in a sentence to help decode words and get meaning from what they read. Just as it is wrong for teachers of whole language to ignore or trivialize phonics, it is also wrong for teachers of phonics to ignore other aspects of the language program. Teachers must always remember that phonemic awareness is very important in learning how to read, especially at the early stages—but it is only a part of the process.

Fortunately for students, most of the words they are introduced to in early reading programs are consistent in their spelling pattern. Generally, these first words are one-syllable words with short vowel sounds in the medial position, such as *run, bed, hand, her,* etc. Words that contain long vowels are generally fairly consistent (*home, year, no, play, keep,* etc.) (Heilman, 1966). Common short words with misleading spelling patterns such as *live, read, come, gone,* and *two,* for example, can easily be taught as sight words without discussing types of vowels.

After students are able to identify all the letters of the alphabet, are able to identify some words by sight, and have experience with using consonant sounds, they are ready for the next step—learning vowel sounds.

Although there is no universal agreement on the exact order in which vowel sounds should be taught, it is generally agreed that it is better to start by introducing short vowel sounds. Some reading programs advocate the teaching of long vowels first because they have the special advantage of sounding like the letter name (Adams, 1998). The major problem with this procedure, however, is that long sounds are often signaled by use of inconsistent vowel digraphs (*say, read, fight, roam, fuel,* etc.) or with an *e* at the end of the word (*home, cape, use,* etc.). Beginning with long vowels thus presents word pattern issues that are better saved for later (Adams, 1998). The reason for starting with short vowels is quite logical—most of the words that students first learn to read contain short vowels. If students have been exposed to consonant sounds and word families, most of the words they have encountered in this context also contain short vowel sounds. Last, short vowels are more regular and less complicated than long vowels and, for that reason alone, are easier to learn. Again, it makes sense to start first with the familiar and less complicated and then proceed from there to the less familiar and more irregular examples.

Figure 5.3

Short Vowels

Aa	Ee	Ii	Oo	Uu
bat	pen	mitt	sock	tub

Long Vowels

Aa	Ee	Ii	Oo	Uu
game	feet	fire	rose	ruler

Every early elementary classroom should have one or more vowel charts that contain not only both the upper- and lowercase vowel letters, but also a picture of an object that represents each vowel sound, so that children can easily identify the vowel with a word containing its sound. The long /a/, for example, would appear on the chart along with a picture representing that sound, such as an *ape*; the short /a/ would appear along with a picture of an *apple*. A second chart depicting the vowel sounds within words—/a/ as in *cake* or *cat*; /e/ as in *hen*, or *ten*, for example— might also be quite useful in providing visual clues for learning these sounds. Although these vowel charts are available at many teachers' stores and other commercial outlets, it would certainly be a great class project to have the students become involved in making their own. They might make a large one for the classroom and another more personal one for themselves. This would be a delightful way to integrate an art class or two with reading activities. Provided it is not overdone, and is done for the right reasons, the more variety and activities we put into reading class, the more meaningful reading becomes for the student. Figure 5.3 is an example of one kind of vowel chart.

SHORT VOWEL SOUNDS

Once students have some visual references, teachers might begin teaching vowel sounds in somewhat the same way they introduced the initial consonants. Starting with the first short vowel phoneme, the teacher writes on the chalkboard a group of words students may already know that contain that sound in the middle position (*cat, man, ham, back, pat,* etc.). She might then ask students to pronounce the words with emphasis on the vowel sound. Have the students spell one of the words and use it in a sentence. Stress that the short sound of /a/ does not sound like the name of the letter *a*. Ask the students to name other words that have the short /a/ sound. Write these words on the board. At this point, the teacher might point out the spelling pattern, noting that when the letter *a* has a consonant before and after it, it has the sound of a short /a/, the same sound as the words listed on the board or chart. However, it is not important to teach rules or generalizations now; students ought to be able observe similarities and internalize certain generalizations on their own.

Figure 5.4 contains listings of one-syllable words with the vowel in the medial position that students may already know or will soon encounter in beginning reading programs. Aside from presenting these words in reading classes, these words are also appropriate for spelling and writing assignments.

Figure 5.4

Short /a/ Sounds

cab	bad	ham	cat	man
jam	sag	rap	tab	mad
tag	lab	Sam	nap	sad
van	Pam	pad	can	map
fat	cap	lap	lad	had
gas	dad	has	wag	rat
nab	lag	ram	zap	lab
bat	hat	sap	mat	vat
dash	pal	had	bag	tan
ran	fan	and	plan	lamp

Short /e/ Sounds

less	dell	set	red	tell
net	bet	wed	hem	jet
bell	men	peg	Ned	pen
fed	leg	yet	ten	vet
red	bed	sell	rest	send
web	Ted	jell	led	met
felt	pet	shell	let	yes
Ben	test	pep	hen	Ken
met	best	wet	hem	zest
pest	went	sell		

Short /i/ Sounds

bit	pit	will	mill	rim
hid	bill	fit	bib	Tim
miss	nip	bid	rich	kid
tip	shin	Jim	hit	till
fix	bid	miss	him	win
rip	kit	lip	bin	wit
lid	tin	kill	rib	hill
fill	kiss	six	fin	lit
sick	skip	pig	Dick	fin
bin	mint	fib	pig	did

(Continued)

(Continued)

Short /o/ Sounds

cot	box	Don	rod	Tom
hop	Bob	pod	job	cod
cob	got	lob	sob	rot
hog	nod	hot	pond	hop
cob	not	pox	lot	bond
rob	rock	jot	fond	pop
dock	dot	mop	lock	hop
pot	cop	got	sod	sob
top	shop	fox	sock	pond
lob	lock			

Short /u/ Sounds

pup	rung	lug	gum	rush
fun	bus	puff	mug	pun
hug	gut	cup	pun	much
dull	hub	bud	sub	mutt
run	bug	hut	fuss	duck
cut	tub	bus	rug	sun
rub	bust	hum	jut	such
must	nut	dud	dug	dust
lush	lull	but	mud	bun
sum	Gus	tug		

Missing Vowels

To make students more aware of vowel sounds, write a short story, or a few sentences from the story, on the board, omitting the vowels. Ask volunteers to read the story according to what they think the words mean. You may also ask the students to write the words on a sheet of paper, supplying the correct vowels. From the popular story "The Little Engine That Could," for example, you could write the following sentence on the board, leaving a space for the proper vowels or vowel digraphs: "Sh_ w_s _ h_pp_ l_ttl_ tr__n f_r sh_ h_d s_ch _ j_lly l__d t_ c_rry." ("She was a happy little train for she had such a jolly load to carry.")

Another variation would be to write a series of longer words on the board without their vowels and then find out how students figure out what each word might mean. Words such as sbtrctn (subtraction), ndrstndng (understanding), and Mchgn (Michigan) make a good challenge for students. This is especially meaningful for later elementary grades.

Playing word detective and finding all the words in a story that have short vowels is another useful activity for identifying vowel sounds. After these words have been identified, they may be placed on a word wall in the classroom for future reference.

LONG VOWEL SOUNDS

As has been stated several times before, there are no perfectly consistent rules for teaching vowel sounds in English. For this reason and others, it is not recommended that generalizations be memorized by the students. It is, on the other hand, desirable and appropriate that the teacher present these generalizations in such a way that students see their application in reading and spelling (Adams, 1998). The teacher, therefore, should know the generalizations well enough to be able to point out these relationships and assist students in applying them when necessary. The most consistent generalizations are listed below.

The Most Consistent Generalizations for Long Vowel Sounds

Long /a/ sound:

- When e appears at the end of a word, the a before it is almost always pronounced as a long /a/: *make, take, fame,* etc.
- When *ay* appears at the end of a word, the *ay* is pronounced as a long /a/: *play, today, may, say,* etc.
- When an *a* is followed by an *i*, the *a* is almost always long and the *i* is almost always silent: *fail, mail, aid, wait,* etc.

Long /e/ sound:

- The long /e/ sound is most often represented by three digraphs: *ee* (*tree, see, deed, peek,* etc.), *ea* (*teach, each, team, weak,* etc.), and *ie* (*grief, thief, piece, niece,* etc.).

- When the digraph *ey* appears at the end of the word, it generally has the long /e/ sound: *jockey, valley, chimney,* etc.
- When the adverbial ending -*ly* is added to a word, the final *y* has the long sound of /e/: *nicely, sadly, willingly, silently,* etc.
- One-syllable words ending in *e* have the long /e/ sound: *me, be, we,* etc.

Long /i/ sound:

- When *e* appears at the end of a word, the /i/ before it is generally long and the final *e* is silent: *nice, wide, tile, ice,* etc.
- When a word contains the combination *igh*, the *g* and the *h* are silent and the /i/ is long: *night, fight, light, bright,* etc.
- When a one-syllable word ends in *y*, it generally has a long /i/ sound: *try, my, sky, buy,* etc. Even when the spelling of *y* changes to *i* when plural and past tense endings are added, it still retains the long /i/ sound: *flies, skies, cried, tried,* etc.
- When the vowel *i* is followed by -*nd*, -*gh*, or -*ld*, it frequently has the long vowel sound.

Long /o/ sound:

- When *e* appears at the end of a word, the /o/ is generally long: *home, note, doze, rose,* etc.
- When the vowel digraph *oa* appears in a word, the /o/ is generally long and the *a* is silent: *boat, oats, foam, coal,* etc.
- When a word ends with *o* or *oe*, it generally has the long /o/ sound: *no, so, toe, tomato,* etc.
- When the vowel *o* is followed by -*ld*, it usually has the long /o/ sound: *old, hold, fold,* etc. The vowel digraph *ow* often has the long /o/ sound: *blow, show, fellow, row,* etc.

Long /u/ sound:

- When *e* appears at the end of a word, the /u/ before it is generally long: *use, mule, dune, cube,* etc.
- When the letter combinations *ew* and *ue* appear at the end of a word, they usually make the long /u/ sound: *new, few, blue, clue, chew,* etc.
- The combination *oo* often has the long /u/ sound: *too, moo, noon, zoom, bloom,* etc.

Although long vowels can be spelled or represented in many uncommon or irregular ways, the vast majority of words fall into several common and regular spelling patterns. Research has shown, for example, that in a sampling of basic words, 85 percent are spelled with complete regularity (Hanna, Hanna, Hodge & Rudolph, 1966). Many consistent alternative spellings of long vowels can be quickly learned and mastered with a little effort. Figure 5.5 shows the primary spelling patterns for each long vowel.

Figure 5.5

Primary Spelling Patterns for Long Vowel Sounds

a–e (a)	-ay (a)	-ai- (a)	-ee- (e)
tame	bay	fail	peep
save	may	jail	beef
rake	ray	mail	feed
cake	way	nail	peek
wage	jay	pail	peel
rave	say	sail	feet
cape	pay	tail	heel
face	day	aid	deep
safe	gay	laid	seed
age	lay	paid	jeep
race	nay	wait	steel
bake	hay	raid	feel

-ea- (e)	-e, -ee (e)	-ie- (e)	-ey (e)
beat	be	brief	galley
leaf	fee	field	key
meal	free	niece	valley
beak	he	priest	kidney
team	Lee	grief	barley
tea	me	fierce	donkey
deal	tree	piece	money
beam	gee	shield	hockey
eat	tee	chief	jockey
heat	bee	wield	monkey
bean	we	pier	chimney
weak	see	thief	turkey

(Continued)

(Continued)

i–e (i)	-y (i)	-ye, -ie (i)	-igh (i)
dice	by	bye	bright
hide	my	rye	light
five	cry	lye	thigh
hike	dry	fries	right
pile	fly	dye	might
dine	ply	eye	high
tide	thy	die	fight
file	sky	vie	sigh
hire	spy	lie	night
lime	fry	pie	sight
wide	pry	tie	plight
mice	shy	eyes	tight

o–e (o)	-oa- (o)	-ow (o)	-o, -oe (o)
home	boat	blow	doe
nose	coal	low	foe
bone	coat	show	go
poke	foam	bow	hoe
doze	goal	own	Joe
cope	goat	row	toe
tone	load	mow	no
hose	loaf	snow	poem
robe	moan	flow	woe
mode	moat	stow	silo
rope	float	tow	so
hope	oath	glow	bingo

u–e (oo)	-ue (oo)	-ew (oo)	-oo (oo)
dude	blue	few	too
huge	clue	dew	zoo
rube	due	drew	zoom
cube	duel	screw	broom
mule	cruel	crew	noon
tune	glue	threw	spoon
duke	hue	blew	soon
use	rue	brew	tooth
rule	Sue	slew	boot
cute	true	new	hoot
dune	fuel	chew	groom

Short to Long

To demonstrate the differences between long and short vowels, write on the board a list of words with short vowels that can be changed into different words with long vowels by adding the letter *e* to the end. Below is a list of some common words that can be changed in this manner. Have students make a list of these kinds of words and display them on the walls of the classroom for occasional review or to add new words as warranted.

VOWEL DIGRAPHS AND DIPHTHONGS

A vowel digraph is the combination of two vowels (graphemes) to represent a single phoneme or sound. The most common vowel digraphs in English are *aw, au, oo, ew, ue,* and *ui.* Two of the digraphs, *ew* and *ue,* contain the long /u/ sound and have already been discussed as part of the spelling pattern for that sound. A third digraph—*ui*—appears with such infrequency (*suit, fruit,* etc.) that it's best to treat words that contain it as sight words. This leaves three of the most common vowel digraphs: *oo, aw,* and *au.*

Two of the digraphs—*aw* and *au*—have the same sound, and *oo* has two distinct sounds: the /oo/ as in *foot* and the /oo/ as in *soon.* Although the generalizations for each sound, like most generalizations, are not always consistent or reliable, they could be of value to students who might be confused about how to spell and write words that contain these sounds, especially the /au/ and /aw/ sound. Certainly the teacher should be aware of them.

Generalizations for *aw* and *au*

- The digraph *au* is generally used at the beginning of some words and in the middle of many others. It is not used at the end of words.
- The digraph *aw* is generally found at the end of a word. When it is not at the end of the word, it often occurs before the letters *k, l,* and n.

See Figure 5.6 for examples for words containing the *aw* and *au* digraphs.

Figure 5.6

Words With *aw* and *au*

aw	au
saw	cause
jaw	pause
paw	caught
straw	daughter
law	auto
lawn	August
claw	author
draw	autumn
crawl	because
raw	saucer
dawn	fault
hawk	Paul

The Digraph *oo*

There are no generalizations regarding the digraph *oo*. A word that contains this digraph can be pronounced in one of two ways: with the long /oo/ as in *loose* and *boot,* or with the short /oo/ as in *hook* and *stood.* No positional clues exist that can be used to direct the student to one pronunciation or the other. Students will need practice discriminating sounds, but it is in the context in which the word is used that they will discover the

Figure 5.7

Words With *oo*

long /oo/ sound	short /oo/ sound
too	took
pool	stood
zoo	look
loop	cook
noon	shook
shoot	brook
tool	book
boost	foot
loose	good
root	wood
tooth	football

proper pronunciation. Figure 5.7 contains examples of words with both pronunciations.

Commercial Games

Many popular games on the market today can be helpful in developing awareness of sounds in words and various spelling patterns for those sounds. These commercial games include Scrabble, Hangman, Word Bingo, and jigsaw puzzles for various age groups. The Phonics Game contains many different card games that can make learning vowel sounds enjoyable. These types of educational games are great to have around the classroom, especially when students cannot go outside for recess or when they have some free time.

Diphthongs

A diphthong is a combination of two vowel sounds, the first gliding into the second to produce one blended sound: the /oi/ as in *boil* and the /ou/ as in *house,* for example. There are four "pure" diphthongs: *ou, oy, oi,* and *ow.* While the diphthongs *oi* and *oy* are always pronounced alike, the

Figure 5.8

Words With Vowel Diphthongs

ou	ow	oi	oy
house	cow	oil	boy
mouse	how	boil	enjoy
count	plow	soil	toy
found	chow	foil	destroy
round	drown	join	Troy
ground	brown	coin	coy
loud	clown	point	alloy
cloud	crowd	choice	Roy
shout	owl	voice	joy
trout	growl	noise	ploy
bounce	prowl	moist	decoy
hour	browse	coil	cowboy

diphthongs *ou* and *ow* are sometimes pronounced alike and sometimes not. The diphthong *ou* is pronounced the same as *ow* in words such as *count, loud, hour,* etc., but it can have another six sounds in words such as *touch, soup, soul, bought, could,* and *famous.* Despite this last problem, a few generalizations or observations about diphthongs can be pointed out that may be helpful in spelling and writing these sounds.

Generalizations About Diphthongs

- When the sound /oi/ or /oy/ is heard at the end of a word, it is generally spelled *oy* (*toy, boy, destroy,* etc.).
- When the sound is heard in the middle of a word, or in a closed position, it is generally spelled *oi* (*boil, noise, voice,* etc.).
- When the /ow/ or /ou/ sound is heard at the end of a word, it is almost always spelled *ow* (*cow, plow,* etc.). See Figure 5.8 for examples of words containing the "pure" diphthongs.

R-CONTROLLED VOWEL SOUNDS

When a vowel is followed by *r,* the sound is neither long nor short, but has a distinctive sound controlled by the *r.* By the time students reach the point

Figure 5.9

Words With *R*-Controlled Vowels

ar	er	or	ir	ur
car	her	for	bird	burn
march	perk	born	girl	burst
hard	fern	cork	third	churn
large	stern	fork	shirt	curl
mark	herd	north	firm	fur
park	were	corn	dirt	hurl
harm	germ	lord	first	hurt
farm	serve	horn	birth	nurse
charm	term	fort	irk	purr
harp	perch	horse	fir	spur
star	clerk	short	sir	turn
tar	ever	torn	flirt	churn

where they may need instruction or practice with words that have a vowel followed by *r*, they have probably already learned many common words that fit this category, such as *her, farm, bird, girl,* etc. They probably learned these words with little or no difficulty and without anyone calling their attention to how the *r* affects the vowel sound. They ought to be able to use and apply that knowledge to other words they may not know that contain a vowel plus *r*. Calling students' attention to certain generalizations regarding vowels plus *r* in the early stages of reading, although certainly not necessary for learning how to read, might be of some benefit down the line.

Generalizations About *R*-Controlled Vowel Sounds

- In many words, a vowel followed by an *r* is long when there is a final *e* at the end of the word: *wire, cure, care,* etc.
- When the word does not have a final *e*, it is usually short: *bird, her, car,* etc. When *ar, er, ir,* and *ur* are followed by a second *r*, the vowel is usually short: *sparrow, error, mirror,* etc.
- When a vowel plus *r* is followed by another vowel, it is usually short: *very, merit, miracle,* etc.

Some of the more frequent *r*-controlled vowels are listed in Figure 5.9. These may be used for board work or seat work exercises.

Word Detective at Home

Here, the teacher might want to play word detective by giving students a chance to find vowel digraphs and diphthongs in one of their textbooks and make a list of them. For a good home activity, ask students to survey the family newspaper to find words that contain certain diphthongs or digraphs. Have Dad and Mom assist, if they want. Students should make a list of the words they find and bring them to the classroom the next day to share with the class. Have the class make a general list and illustrate it with pictures that represent the words. The illustrated list can be displayed in the classroom.

Mind Reading

Consider playing mind reading with the class. Get up in front of the class and give students two clues to the word you are thinking of. Begin by saying something like "I'm thinking of a word that rhymes with *glue* and is not a falsehood." "I am thinking of something that has *ur* in the middle and is a very slow animal." After directing the activity a couple of times you may hand a student a list of words you want to review. The student chooses a word from the list and gives two clues to the class. The first to get the correct answer receives the list and chooses the next word, and so on.

HOMONYMS

A homonym (a more exact term is homophone) is a word that sounds identical to another word but has a different meaning and spelling. Consideration of homonyms at this point is logical because, with the exception of a few words, most of the problems with homonyms come from trying to determine which alternative spelling of the vowel is appropriate in a particular written usage (Furness, 1990).

One of the peculiarities of English is that it contains pairs of words (homographs) that can be spelled exactly the same (*row–row, read–read, object–object,* etc.) but differ in meaning and pronunciation. At the same time, other words (homophones or homonyms) have the same pronunciation but are spelled differently with entirely different meanings (*to–too–two, blew–blue, so–sew,* etc.). In the first instance, one cannot tell just by looking at the word which meaning to use; in the second instance, one cannot tell just from the pronunciation what word to write. Even after many years of schooling, it is not uncommon for literate adults to habitually confuse spellings of homonyms, writing *there* instead of *their* or writing *to* instead of *too*.

Figure 5.10

Common Homonyms

to–too–two	there–their	hear–here	blue–blew
I–eye	dear–deer	red–read	flower–flour
ate–eight	so–sew–sow	see–sea	new–knew
know–no	week–weak	beet–beat	for–four
son–sun	reign–rain	air–heir	misses–Mrs.
which–witch	write–right	hour–our	cell–sell
die–dye	way–weigh	sail–sale	seem–seam
days–daze	by–buy–bye	lead–led	meat–meet
pair–pare	cellar–seller	pail–pale	principal–principle
night–knight	cent–sent	be–bee	peace–piece
do–due–dew	bare–bear	ant–aunt	break–brake
feet–feat	made–maid	one–won	some–sum

Homonyms, near-homonyms, and words that contain unnecessary silent letters are the basis of spelling demon lists and present a real challenge for teacher and students. There is just no logical way for the student to learn these words except to become aware of the more common ones and to practice spelling them and using them in conversation and writing. Figure 5.10 is a list of some of the more common homonyms met by students in the early elementary grades. It is extremely important for students' educational advancement and self-esteem that they learn not only how to spell these words, but also how to use them properly in written sentences. Being able to spell and write these words in proper context is a sure sign of spelling and writing accomplishment.

Missing Homonyms

Homonyms generally do not pose as much of a problem in reading as they do in spelling. Many adults still write *to* for *too, principal* for *principle, break* for *brake,* and so forth. For this reason it is good to give the students plenty of written work along with their reading material. Many teachers will reproduce sentences that have the homonym removed.

Students are to supply the proper word. For example:

John _____ what he was doing. (new, knew)

She was told to wait one _____. (hour, our)

Dad would like to _____ some bread. (by, buy, bye)

Mr. Smith is a nice _____. (principle, principal)

The children put _____ books over _____. (there, their)

Homonym Pictures

Drawing pictures to represent homonyms is also a challenge. Let students use their imagination to produce pictures to illustrate the differences between the two words. They might draw a picture of someone's hair and a hare running in the field. They might draw a picture of a pile of books with the caption "their books" and a picture of a boy standing in the corner with the caption "standing there in the corner." Challenge students to draw one picture that illustrates both homonyms: "Their books are over there in the corner." "Hey! That hare has hair!" Collect the students' word pictures and display them in the classroom.

SIGHT WORDS

Sight words are words that, because of some kind of irregularity in spelling or pronunciation, are thought to be better learned by sight, rather than trying to sound them out phonemically. About two hundred of the most common words used in English (*the, two, done, gone, are, have,* etc.) fit into this category, yet they make up about two-thirds of the words used in print (Furness, 1990).

Students can learn to recognize all kinds of consistent spelling patterns and all kinds of rules and generalizations that may assist them in learning new words, yet there comes a time when spelling patterns and generalizations fail. Patterns and rules simply cannot help students pronounce common words such as *laugh, love, one, two, said,* etc. In fact, attempting to apply rules to irregular words is one of the reasons good readers are sometimes poor spellers, whereas good spellers are rarely poor readers.

Aside from their irregularities, there is another reason to learn many words as sight words: While these words are common, they are so often misspelled that they require some special attention. Particular idiosyncrasies of each word, such as double letters, silent letters, and unconventional spellings, should be pointed out. If necessary, students should be given special practice or opportunities to write these words. Whereas invented spellings may be helpful during writing assignments so students can get their ideas on paper, eventually they will have to confront their difficulties with conventional spelling. Invented spelling should be only a temporary solution.

Around the World

A popular way to help children learn sight words quickly is to play Around the World. This activity can be used to learn number facts and multiplication tables as well as sight words. Print the words you want the students to identify by sight on large cards in print large enough for the students to see at a short distance. Place them in a pile so that only the top word is exposed. Have the children line up in single row along the side of the classroom. Have the first student in line stand next to the second student, and then uncover the first word. The first child to say the flashed word moves to the side of the next student in line. The one who didn't respond, or responded too slowly, takes that space in line. Again the teacher flashes a new word. Each time, the student who says the word first gets to move down the line. If there is any doubt about who said the word first, the teacher declares a tie and the same students are given another chance. The object of the game is to be the first person to go around the class and arrive at his or her original position in line.

CONCLUSION

From the contents of this chapter, the reader can easily discern how complicated the process of teaching reading by using the sound-symbol system can be. As we have seen in the last chapter, consonants are somewhat regular while "the conduct of vowels is just plain disorderly" (Adams, 1998, p. 118). Yet, aside from a complete alphabet reform, there is no way of getting around learning the vowels. There are only six primary vowels, but they appear in every word and syllable in the language, and they account for roughly 39 percent of the character space in English (Mayzner & Tresselt, 1966).

Whereas only a couple of consonants have more than one sound, every single one of the vowels, by itself or in combination with another vowel (vowel digraph), can take on many different vowel sounds. A beginning teacher focusing on just this aspect of phonics might become quickly discouraged at the prospect.

However, although vowel sounds are many and varied, they are nonetheless highly consistent within certain patterns. Through practice with phonograms or word families and familiarity with the examples in this chapter, students can learn basic skills in sounding out and spelling vowels that will help them read and spell and figure out more advanced and less familiar words.

When students reach the point where they are ready for instruction in the more advanced vowel sounds, they will have already been exposed to sounds that will lay the foundation, have developed a more advanced active and passive vocabulary, and have had plenty of previous practice. Previous mastery of one skill makes it easier to master more advanced skills and understandings. The more practice and exposure students receive, the more they will internalize these rules or skills, the faster they can process print, and the more they concentrate on meaning rather than pronunciation. This chapter has attempted to demonstrate the importance of teaching reading, spelling, and writing together for the sake of reinforcement. Most of the mistakes students make in spelling or writing have to do with vowel sounds. This is seen regularly in students' attempts at invented spelling. That's why it is essential to attempt to integrate the examples in this chapter as much as possible into the regular spelling class and find activities and games that involve reading, writing, and spelling. The language arts should be taught in such a way that all three disciplines reinforce each other.

6

Teaching Syllabication and Word Structure Skills

The first words a child learns to read are generally one-syllable singular nouns (*dog, house, mom,* etc.) and present-tense verbs (*look, run, come,* etc.). It doesn't take very long, however, before beginning readers encounter longer and more complicated words (*arithmetic, geography, Washington,* etc.), together with changes both at the beginning and ending of the word that alter the word's meaning in some way (*boy–boys; look–looking; happy–unhappy;* etc.). Later on, as the student advances from reader to reader or grade to grade, the words become ever more involved and complicated, in both structure and meaning. Generally, it is not until about the fourth grade that "normal readers begin to perceive syllables more quickly and accurately than single letters" (Freidrich et al., 1979, cited in Adams, 1998, p. 125).

The first time students use a computer for anything other than games, they are handicapped by the fact that using a computer means learning a "new" language with a strange vocabulary all its own (*database, spreadsheet,* etc.). If they want to do more than just punch keys and move a mouse, they are forced to learn this strange language. When students look at a map of the United States, they find myriad strange-sounding words such as *Menominee, Okeechobee, Kalamazoo, Tallahassee, Chiricahua,* and hundreds of other polysyllabic names of towns and cities. When students attempt to read the directions on how to assemble parts of a kite or look up the football scores in the local newspapers, again they face special challenges with longer technical and unfamiliar words. Their ability mentally to divide words into syllables and to sound them out is key to their ability to read and pronounce this challenging new vocabulary. Because of their knowledge of spelling patterns, "skilled readers break long words down into syllabic units. They do so automatically and in the very course of perceiving them" (Adams, 1998, p. 123).

THE NEED FOR SYLLABICATION SKILLS

The word challenge never seems to stop. The more exposure students have to reading material and the more they develop their reading skills, the more complicated the words become both in structure and meaning. Without the ability to mentally divide words into syllables in order to get to the pronunciation (or at least the approximate pronunciation), little progress would be made in reading (Adams, 1998).

The ability to divide unfamiliar words into syllables is not only a necessary tool for children, but plays an important part in adult learning as well. When learning a foreign language, for example, the ability to divide new words into syllables in order to sound them out is essential. When teachers take the roll call of new students for the first time in the classroom, the only clue to how to pronounce some of their names is to (mentally) divide the name into syllables and hope for the best.

Not only do foreign languages and computers have a language all their own, but so do medicine, law, religion, science, and most other areas of learning. Although the average person requires knowledge of only several thousand words for writing, and perhaps another ten thousand to twenty thousand more for reading, the English language has six hundred thousand words and proper names (Furness, 1990). As one linguist put it, this abundance of "scientific, legal, technical, artistic, and philosophical terms makes English the richest and most expansive tongue in the world" (Furness, 1990, p. 67). To be knowledgeable and fluent in these areas, we must first master the vocabulary. And to master the vocabulary, we must be able to read it.

RULES FOR DIVIDING WORDS INTO SYLLABLES

As has been stated several times before, English has so few high-percentage phonemic rules or generalizations that it is generally a bad idea to require children to memorize them (Clymer, 1963). When it comes to the rules for dividing words into syllables, however, one might consider making an exception. Unlike most of the other rules and generalizations we have seen, rules for dividing words into syllables are very consistent, can be easily learned, and, with practice, can become internalized without a great deal of stress or frustration. If memorization of these rules still seems like a bad idea, then the teacher should, at least, provide the class with enough experiences and practice so that the rules become internalized over a period of time.

Learning the rules and getting sufficient practice in applying them teaches much more than just the sounds of the words. Students are also learning to look at the structure of the English language and how words are put together. They learn not only how vowels and consonants affect the sounds of words, but they also kearn about root words and how prefixes and suffixes change the meaning of words. They are exposed to tense changes in English and inflectional endings, which will ultimately help them write more grammatically accurate sentences and assist in developing better spelling habits. Certainly, it is important that students learn and become familiar with the principles underlying these rules.

Syllabication Rules and Examples

- There are as many syllables as there are vowel sounds. It is the vowel sound that is important, not the number of vowels. For example, the word *pan* has one vowel and one vowel sound. The word *pain* has two vowels and only one vowel sound. *Cheese* has three vowels and one vowel sound.
- Compound words are divided between the two words: *sun-shine, cow-boy, basket-ball,* etc. If further division is necessary, then they follow the general rules below.
- Divide syllables between double consonants (VC-CV): *Sun-day, run-ner, tar-dy,* etc.
- When a single consonant comes between two vowels and the first vowel is long, the consonant generally goes with the second vowel (V-CV): *pa-per, so-ber, tu-lip,* etc.
- When a single consonant comes between two vowels and the first vowel is short, the consonant generally goes with the first vowel (VC-V): *cab-in, met-al, col-or,* etc.
- When a word ends in *-ble, -cle, -dle, -gle, -kle, -ple, -tle,* or *-zle,* this combination forms the final syllable: *an-kle, can-dle, amica-ble,* etc.
- When a word contains a consonant blend or digraph, keep the combination together when dividing the word: *ma-chines, teach-er, coun-try,* etc.
- One-syllable prefixes and suffixes generally form a separate syllable: *re-new, un-like-ly, pre-heat-ed,* etc.

The rules above are fairly consistent and can be internalized by the students with additional practice and review every now and then.

Figures 6.1–6.8 contain groupings of familiar words to which each rule applies. Students may use these lists to practice dividing words into syllables. After reviewing these words, in order to insure that the class receives sufficient practice seeing how the rules apply, follow up by having the students discover other words from their textbooks, newspapers, or magazines that follow the rules. Syllabication rules can also be put to good use in spelling lessons.

Figure 6.1

Rule 1: There are as many syllables as there are vowel sounds. Generally, when an *e* appears at the end of a word, it is silent. Generally, when two vowels come together, they produce only one vowel sound.

I = one vowel, one sound
Have = two vowels, one sound
Teacher = three vowels, two sounds
Understanding = four vowels, four sounds
Hydrophobia = five vowels, five sounds

Figure 6.2

Rule 2: Compound words are divided between the two words.

sand-box	blue-bird	book-mark	ant-hill
dog-house	road-way	eye-lid	air-line
life-boat	frost-bite	fire-wood	short-stop
green-house	wild-cat	sail-boat	grand-ma
shell-fish	cook-book	sun-light	note-book
bird-house	pan-cake	hard-ball	water-fall
rain-bow	moon-light	wind-mill	side-walk
in-door	drug-store	wash-room	fire-fly
spot-light	house-boat	farm-house	bath-room
air-plane	wish-bone	key-hole	lock-out
life-time	door-bell	hay-stack	foot-ball
out-field	pig-tail	tip-toe	gold-fish
black-bird	down-town	tooth-pick	sun-light

Figure 6.3

Rule 3: Divide syllables between double consonants.

let-ter	con-tact	cen-ter	tar-dy
an-gel	tur-nip	mar-vel	pen-cil
sup-per	can-dy	ar-my	part-ner
in-sect	her-mit	swim-mer	bas-ket
bar-rel	run-ner	un-der	doc-tor
mit-ten	dol-lar	el-bow	lit-tle
dad-dy	cop-per	cor-ner	sil-ver
sug-gest	rub-ber	don-key	wal-rus
fun-ny	cir-cus	har-bor	chim-ney
val-ley	car-rot	but-ton	rib-bon
lad-der	pic-nic	les-son	gram-mar
gar-den	sil-ly	car-go	nap-kin

Figure 6.4

Rule 4: When a single consonant comes between two vowels and the first vowel is long, the single consonant generally goes with the second vowel.

lo-cal	be-gan	A-pril	pa-per
o-pen	ro-ver	so-lar	cra-zy
tu-lip	so-da	fi-nal	o-ver
ha-zel	va-cate	mo-tor	Chi-na
po-ny	li-lac	ze-bra	vi-tal
gro-cer	clo-ver	fe-male	se-cret
ti-dy	ti-ger	fe-ver	ma-ple
hu-mor	a-gent	I-vy	dri-ver
la-dy	la-bor	fi-ner	wi-per
pi-rate	be-gin	vo-ter	vo-cal

Figure 6.5

Rule 5: When a single consonant comes between two vowels and the first vowel is short, the consonant generally goes with the first vowel.

doz-en	fin-ish	cit-y	stud-y
vis-it	lin-en	riv-er	at-om
sev-en	mod-el	liz-ard	bus-y
lem-on	ev-er	grav-el	pan-ic
nev-er	pris-on	driv-en	trav-el
bod-y	cab-in	heav-en	vow-el
tow-el	col-or	prop-er	giv-en
met-al	pan-el	Sen-ate	liv-er
hab-it	jur-y	civ-ic	viv-id
wag-on	giv-ing	clev-er	ov-en

Figure 6.6

Rule 6: When a word ends in *-ble, -cle, -dle, -gle, -kle, -ple, -tle,* or *-zle,* this combination forms the final syllable.

ma-ple	bub-ble	ta-ble	ca-ble
lit-tle	set-tle	ap-ple	dan-gle
drib-ble	cat-tle	rat-tle	ea-gle
nee-dle	han-dle	fraz-zle	peo-ple
noo-dle	spar-kle	grum-ble	min-gle
un-cle	cir-cle	daz-zle	poo-dle
bat-tle	an-gle	hur-dle	ri-fle
gen-tle	cas-tle	trou-ble	fiz-zle
pur-ple	crum-ble	pad-dle	bot-tle
sim-ple	muz-zle	waf-fle	gig-gle
bu-gle	an-kle	fid-dle	han-dle

Figure 6.7

Rule 7: When a word contains a consonant blend or digraph, keep the combination together when dividing the word.

teach-er	im-prove	preach-er	ham-ster
im-ply	con-clude	sim-pler	ath-lete
in-struct	de-gree	re-strict	im-press
chil-dren	ex-treme	in-ter-pret	se-cret
An-drew	weath-er	pro-gram	Pil-grims
sur-prise	meth-od	noth-ing	wheth-er
mo-ther	cel-e-brate	ma-chine	a-gree
coun-try	sub-tract	de-ploy	sam-pler
hun-dred	En-glish	re-place	tel-e-scope
dis-play	broth-er	im-plore	feath-er

Figure 6.8

Rule 8: One-syllable prefixes and suffixes generally form a separate syllable.

pro-noun	ex-plore	co-ed	un-friend-ly
thick-ness	im-plant	mis-place	ill-ness
un-like-ly	re-ac-tion	pro-long	un-wise
quick-ness	home-less	fore-cast	dent-ist
pro-tect-ing	un-do	glow-ing-ly	dress-es
mis-use	mid-way	mid-night	poor-ly
un-trust-ing	pre-view	de-cod-ing	non-sense
art-ful-ness	un-grate-ful	dis-taste-ful	hav-ing
land-ed	care-ful-ly	pay-ment	dis-trust

Once students learn the rules, the teacher might encourage them to invent their own words for practice. Dividing nonsense words, such as *tackatokie, ambridorcodill,* or *unfestatoral,* into syllables can be a challenging way to practice this skill. Locating four-, five-, and six-syllable words in newspapers and magazines can also be helpful. Giving a prize to the student who finds the longest word in the newspaper is another way of promoting curiosity about words and their meanings. Dividing words into syllables need not be an onerous task.

It is important to give all students enough practice dividing words into syllables so that they can apply the skill when necessary. For young children just beginning to read, some exposure to these rules, as the need occurs, is generally sufficient. For more advanced students and older students who may need extra help, taking time out every now and then to discuss specific rules and giving them words to practice can be very help-ful. As has been pointed out before, learning syllabication skills not only helps children learn the sounds of words, but also allows the teacher opportunities to discuss such topics as parts of speech, root words, the meaning of prefixes and suffixes, and comparatives, superlatives, and pos-sessives as these features occur in longer words. Discussions can become lively as students try to divide and sound out unfamiliar words such as *discombobulate* or *zoogeography.* Students soon learn there is more to words than just sounds.

Dictionary Search

Pass out a dictionary to each member of the class and ask who can find the longest word. Give them a few minutes and then discuss the words they've found. You might ask students to find ten words with eight or more letters and write them down. Again after a period of time stop and discuss the words. A vari-ation on this activity would be to find words with four, five, or six syllables. As an afterschool activity you might ask the students to go home that night and find the longest word they can in the newspaper and write the sentence in which it appears. The words, their pronunciation, and their meaning could be dis-cussed in class the next morning.

Word Wall

Appoint a different student each day to write on a class-room wallboard one polysyllabic word he or she discovers in the course of the school day. Students will likely add words like *geography, arithmetic, multiplication, Mississippi,* etc. At the end of the week discuss the words on the wall chart.

PREFIXES AND SUFFIXES

One of the major clues for unlocking polysyllabic words is knowledge of prefixes and suffixes (which taken together are called affixes) and how they affect the meanings of words. A prefix is defined as a syllable or syllables added to the beginning of a word to change its meaning (*new–renew, happy–unhappy*, etc.). A suffix is defined as a syllable or syllables added to the ending of a word to change its meaning (*girl–girls, poor–poorly, good–goodness*, etc.). A prefix added to a word makes it a new word, often with a quite different or even opposite meaning (*happy–unhappy, obey–disobey*, etc.). Suffixes added to the ending of a word can also change the meaning of the root word (*hope–hopeless, teach–teacher*, etc.). More often, however, suffixes change the grammatical function of the word (*do–doing, happy–happily*, etc.). Knowledge of the meanings of prefixes and suffixes not only assists in the structural analysis of words and syllabication, but is also a great help for improving comprehension and spelling skills.

Unfortunately for elementary teachers, English contains such an abundance of both prefixes and suffixes that it is almost impossible and certainly impractical to expose children to a large proportion of them. Fortunately, most prefixes and suffixes are so rare that they can be discarded as meaningless at this level. One study gives examples of almost one hundred and fifty different prefixes and ninety different suffixes (Fry, Kress, & Fountoukidis, 1993). Many of the prefixes—such as *giga-* (billion), *tetra-* (four), and *ennea-* (nine)—are rare, as are many of the suffixes. So rare are they that it's doubtful whether many educated adults would be able to identify and explain even half of these affixes.

Students are exposed at a very early level to words such as *unhappy, going, remake,* and others that have a prefix or suffix. As they progress in reading ability they are exposed to more involved prefixes and suffixes. At times they will ask questions about additions, or they will need some instruction from their teacher.

It is important that the teacher point out to students that not all words that start with what looks like a prefix do indeed have one—the *un-* in *uncle,* the *re-* in *relative,* and the *mis-* in *mission,* for example. In fact, about 15 to 20 percent of the words students encounter in reading share this complexity (White, Swell, & Yanagehara, 1989, cited in Blevins, 1998). Teachers should also point out that different prefixes can express the same meaning. For example, *in-, im-, ir-,* and *il-* can mean *not; contra-* and *anti-* mean *against; bi-* and *di-* mean *two.* These fine distinctions, however, need not be presented until the student is ready. Introduction of these can be held off until the third, fourth, or fifth grade and beyond.

Figures 6.9 and 6.10 contain lists of the twenty most common prefixes and suffixes, based on the *American Heritage Word Frequency Book* (Carrol, Davies, & Richman, 1971). They are listed in order of frequency.

When to Teach Prefixes and Suffixes

There is no exact order in which prefixes and suffixes ought to be taught. Rather than just teaching them for the sake of teaching them, however, it

Figure 6.9   Common Prefixes

Prefix Meaning Examples

Prefix	Meaning	Examples
un-	not	unhappy, unlike
re-	again	renew, retry, redo
in-, im-, ir-, il-	not	inactive, impossible, irregular, illegal
dis-	opposite of	distrust, disobey
en-, em-	cause to	enclose, embrace
non-	not, not one	nonsense, nonactive
in-, im-	into	inhale, implant
over-	too much	overstate, overkill
mis-	bad	misspell, mislay
sub-	under	submerge, subject
pre-	before	preplan, prepay
inter-	between	interstate, intersect
fore-	before	forethought, foregone
de-	opposite of	debase, detoxify
trans-	across	transport, transmit
super-	excess, above	superman, supervise
semi-	half	semipublic, semicircle
anti-	against	antiwar, antibody
mid-	middle	midyear, midtown
under-	too little	underdone, undercook

would be more practical and timely to wait until there is a particular need and the timing seems appropriate. For example, after the student (or reading group) finishes reading a story that contains several common prefixes, the teacher might take a little time to talk about the role of prefixes and suffixes. Using the examples the student just read in the book, and with their meanings still fresh in mind, the teacher would then have a great opportunity to present other words the student may or may not know that have

Figure 6.10 Common Suffixes

Suffix Meaning Examples

Suffix	Meaning	Examples
-s, -es	more than one	cats, foxes
-ed (-/d/, -/t/)	past tense	snowed, looked
-ing	verb ending	going, singing
-ly	like	nicely, joyfully
-er, -or	one who does	singer, actor
-tion, -sion	state of	action, division
-able, -ible	capable of	lovable, sensible
-al, -ial	pertaining to	musical, racial
-y	quality of	fruity, rainy
-ness	condition of	sadness, goodness
-ity, -ty	quality of	eternity, safety
-ment	action or process	judgment, development
-ic	pertaining to	phonetic, comic
-ous, -ious	having quality of	humorous, mysterious
-en	become, made of	darken, wooden
-er	comparative	nicer, softer
-ive	state of being	active, attractive
-ful	full of	delightful, helpful
-less	without	sugarless, mindless
-est	superlative	highest, kindest

similar prefixes and suffixes. Teaching concepts about similar prefixes and suffixes when the opportunity presents itself makes the teaching more relevant and the learning more likely to be retained and applied.

Specific instruction on the meanings of certain prefixes and suffixes and how these additions change the meaning of words can be given in most areas of the curriculum. In a geography class, for example, students might read how Magellan circumnavigated the globe. This could lead to a discussion and investigation of the prefix *circum-* and its meaning. Other words, such as *circumstance, circumscribe, circulation,* and their meanings, could be brought up in the discussion to further understanding of this prefix. In English class, the teacher might want to present specific lessons and exercises on how to form plurals (*boy–boys, box–boxes, lady–ladies,* etc.), or present lessons on comparatives and superlatives of adjectives (*tall–taller–tallest, small–smaller–smallest,* etc.), or practice the tenses of verbs (*walk– walked–walking, need–needed–needing,* etc.). (In these instances, English class, rather than reading class, would be a more appropriate setting for teaching how prefixes and suffixes affect the meaning of words.) Math class offers all kinds of opportunities to present, talk about, and give examples of the many prefixes that are used in the words for number and shape (*triangle, pentagon, diameter, circumference,* etc.). Since so many common spelling mistakes (*pervent, loveing, nashun, runing,* etc.) are the result of a poor understanding of prefixes and suffixes and how they operate, it would be beneficial to spend several spelling classes going over the meanings and applications of the more common ones.

Rules for Suffixes

When adding a prefix to a word, generally no spelling changes are involved, no doubling of consonants, no changing letters to other letters, and virtually no rules or generalizations to be learned. This makes them quite a bit easier to learn and remember than suffixes, which get tangled up in generalizations and exceptions. The inability to handle suffixes is one of the major causes of spelling problems. Not only is it important to spend time on suffixes in reading classes, but special practice and instruction must also be extended in spelling and language course work. Learning suffixes takes time and plenty of practice.

Below are some of the rules for adding suffixes to words. As with the suffixes themselves, the rules may be taught or pointed out when the occasion presents itself.

- When a word ends in *e,* drop the *e* before a suffix that begins with a vowel: *sale–salable, come–coming, nerve–nervous.* Exception: when the final *e* is preceded by *c* or *g,* the *e* is retained to preserve the soft sound: *peace–peaceable, change–changeable.*
- When a word ends in *e,* keep the *e* before a suffix that begins with a consonant: *sure–surely, active–actively, care–careless.* Three common exceptions are *judgment, ninth,* and *truly.*
- When a word ends in *y* preceded by a consonant, change the *y* to *i* before adding the suffix: *plenty–plentiful, glory–glorious, happy–happily.* Exception: Do not change the *y* to *i* if the suffix begins with *i: carry–carrying.* Do not change the *y* to *i* if the *y* is preceded by a vowel: *joy–joyful.*
- When a one-syllable word ends in a consonant preceded by a vowel, double the consonant: *run–runner, spin–spinner, bet–betting.* Exception: words with two vowels before the single consonant do not double the consonant: *seat–seated, rain–rained.*

- When a word has more than one syllable, double the consonant only if the accent of the word is on the last syllable: *admit–admitted, compel–compelling, begin–beginning.* Exceptions to the rule include words that have two vowels before the single consonant (*repeat–repeated, defeat–defeated)* and words ending in two consonants (*result–resulting, hard–harder).* Words not accented on the last syllable do not double the consonant: *open–opened, benefit–benefited.*
- When a word ends in *c*, insert *k* to retain the hard sound of the *c* before adding a suffix that begins with *e*, *i*, or *y*: *picnic–picnicking, panic–panicking.*

Prefix Puzzles

An activity that will help to teach prefixes and suffixes and how they change meaning is to have the students copy a list of words from the board that contains several different prefixes. Pass out strips of heavyweight construction paper. Have students copy the words onto the construction paper. Pass out scissors and then instruct students how and where to cut off the prefix from the root word. Have the students cut off the prefixes, mix the word parts up on their desk, and then put the prefixes back where they belong. Students will find they can create words not on the original list by switching prefixes. Have the students save the pieces in a large envelope. The next day add another five words with the same prefixes and have them do the same thing. Ask students to mix these new words with the old and then match prefixes with root words. Every once in a while add some new words to the mix.

Try the same activity with the suffixes. Students will find it more difficult to create new words because of the changes induced in the root words by the suffixes.

FORMING PLURALS

Today, when one looks at a highly inflectional language like Latin, with its seemingly endless lists of conjugations and declensions, one wonders how our grandparents ever got through those classes. One of the first lessons they learned was that Latin was not one bit like English in its structure. Whereas English is relatively free in its word order and with very few endings, Latin is very rigid and exact. Unlike English, where we only have to worry about singular and plural forms of the noun, those studying Latin have to learn that a noun can have four different types of endings, and that these endings change according to how the noun is used in the sentence. If Latin students get over the hurdle of learning all these noun forms and changes, they are then confronted with the even more complicated changes to Latin verbs, which can seem almost impossible for the average student to learn and understand.

At the other extreme, English has few inflectional endings. A singular noun (*girl, house, cat*) is always spelled the same way whether it is the subject of the sentence, the object of the sentence, or the object of a preposition. The only time inflectional endings are added to nouns is to show plurality and possession: *The cats died. This is Mary's house.*

Although a few nouns in English have the same spelling for both the singular and plural forms (*deer, sheep, trout,* etc.) and a few words have irregular plurals (*foot–feet, woman–women, ox–oxen,* etc.), the vast majority of plurals are formed by adding either *-s* or *-es* to the singular ending (*boy–boys, cat–cats, branch–branches, dress–dresses,* etc.).

Although these two plural endings are spelled with an *s*, they generally are pronounced as /z/. The only time s retains its /s/ sound is when it follows *f, k, p,* or *t* (*cliffs, bricks, lamps, pots,* etc.). Children are so used to words ending in *s* with the /z/ sound that they rarely need help with this observation.

Below are the generalizations for adding plural endings to words. Becoming aware of these generalizations, while not a great help in learning to read, is essential for correct spelling. So many of the simple spelling mistakes children and adults often make reflect a poor knowledge of these generalizations. Practice with these generalizations, while not a cure-all for most spelling problems, can go a long way toward developing better spelling practices and a more mature understanding of how our language operates.

Generalizations for Forming Plurals

- The plural of most nouns is formed by adding *-s* to the singular noun. The s has the sound of /s/ when preceded by *f, k,* p, or *t*: *lamps, cats, cliffs, books.* In all other cases the s has the sound of /z/: *cars, girls, trains.*
- The plural of nouns that end in *ss, ch, sh,* and *x* is formed by adding *-es* to the ending of the word: *glasses, churches, dishes, foxes.*
- When a noun ends in *y* preceded by a consonant, change the *y* to *i* and add *-es: flies, armies, skies.*
- When a noun ends in *y* preceded by a vowel, generally add *-s* without changing the final *y* to *i: alleys, chimneys, forays, boys.*
- When a noun ends in *o* preceded by a consonant, generally *-es* is added to form the plural: *cargoes, potatoes, tornadoes.*
- When a noun ends in *f* or *fe,* often the *f* or *fe* is changed to *ves* to form the plural. This usually takes place when the *f* or *fe* is preceded by a long vowel or by *l: calves, shelves, lives, loaves.* Nouns ending in *ff* usually just add *-s.* Warning: Since this generalization has so many exceptions, it is a good idea to consult a dictionary when in doubt.
- Some exceptions to the generalization include *belief–beliefs, brief–briefs, dwarf–dwarfs, proof–proofs, roof–roofs, chief–chiefs,* and *reef–reefs.*
- Some nouns have irregular plural endings: *bison–bison, child–children, deer–deer, foot–feet, goose–geese, man–men, moose–moose, mouse–mice, tooth–teeth, woman–women, sheep–sheep, swine–swine,* etc.

- Most nouns that come from a foreign language have become anglicized in pronunciation and form their plurals according to the generalizations above. Some words, however, form their plurals by retaining their foreign form. This is especially true of many words with Latin origins. Few of these words are likely to be encountered in elementary school reading materials. Some of the more common ones include *alumna–alumnae, alumnus–alumni, medium–media, datum–data, curriculum–curricula, oasis–oases, focus–foci, madame–mesdames, minimum–minima, maximum–maxima, vertebra–vertebrae, nucleus–nuclei.*

Plural Practice

Since such variation exists in how plurals are formed, students will need a great deal of practice writing the various plural forms. You may from time to time want to put a list of nouns on the board or pass out a list to the class of words that end in *-s, -ss, -ch, -sh,* and *-x* and ask them to change these words into plurals. You may do the same with nouns ending in *-y,* having the students change *y* to *i* and add *-es.* Have them write original sentences using the plurals they have made. For future reference, consider placing these plural words with the endings underlined on a wall chart. When students learn to spell a word in a spelling lesson— *candy, dress, house,* etc.—you can point out what changes need to be made, if any, in learning the plural form. Students could be encouraged to learn both forms together. Write a story or a few sentences, or have students write a story, then ask students to rewrite it changing singulars to plurals and plurals to singular.

CONTRACTIONS

A contraction is two words written together with one or more letters missing. The missing letter or letters are replaced by an apostrophe. Since contractions result from major changes in the structure of the word, they should be taught as sight words or by other means, rather than by trying to sound them out.

There are three general types of contractions: those involving simple verb forms with *not* (*aren't, won't, isn't*); those involving pronouns with verbs (*we're, it'll, you've*); and those where *-'s* or *-'d* stands for the verb *is, had, has,* or *would* (*she's, I'd, who's*). Students should be given enough practice using these words in written sentences so that they eventually become natural and pose few problems either in writing or spelling. Figures 6.11–6.13 give examples of common contractions.

Figure 6.11

Verb + n't (not)

aren't (are not)	don't (do not)	shouldn't (should not)
can't (can not)	hadn't (had not)	wasn't (was not)
couldn't (could not)	hasn't (has not)	weren't (were not)
didn't (did not)	haven't (have not)	won't (would not)
doesn't (does not)	isn't (is not)	wouldn't (would not)

Figure 6.12

Pronoun + Shortened Verb

we're (we are)	I'll (I will, I shall)	I've (I have)
you're (you are)	he'll (he will)	we've (we have)
they're (they are)	she'll (she will)	you've (you have)
	we'll (we will)	they've (they have)
	you'll (you will)	
	they'll (they will)	
	it'll (it will)	
	that'll (that will)	

CONCLUSION

Next to learning the letters of the alphabet and associated sounds, the second most important skill students need to learn is how to divide words into syllables. Too many times a student who is insecure in reading will look at the first syllable of a polysyllabic word and then guess the rest of the syllables. Such a student is apt to read *remember* for *reminder, important* for *importing, generals* for *generalizations,* etc. Other students just shake their head and don't try at all.

It is important that students learn that a polysyllabic word is just a long word made up of sounds they probably already know or can figure out easily. Students do not necessarily have to learn the rules for dividing words into syllables as presented in this book. It is important, however, for

Figure 6.13

-'s or -'d for Is, Has, Had, or Would

-'s (is, has)	-'d (had, would)
he's (he is, he has)	I'd (I had, I would)
she's (she is, she has)	he'd (he had, he would)
here's (here is)	she'd (she had, she would)
it's (it is)	we'd (we had, we would)
that's (that is, that has)	you'd (you had, you would)
there's (there is, there has)	they'd (they had, they would)
what's (what is, what has)	that'd (that had, that would)
where's (where is, where has)	there'd (there had, there would)
who's (who is, who has)	

them to learn and remember that every syllable must have a vowel sound. If students keep the vowels separated and the blends together, they have a good chance of coming close, or close enough, to the actual pronunciation to get the word correct.

Although the general rule should be to teach skills in the context of reading and as needed, it is a good idea now and then to set aside a specific time devoted just to teaching some of the skills in this chapter—a block of time for syllabication, a block of time for plurals, etc. Since syllabication and word analysis skills will have relevance for spelling and writing, it is also useful from time to time to tie these activities into one larger language arts project. Last, let us remember that, even in the twenty-first century, the old Latin adage "Repetitio est mater studiorum" (Repetition is the mother of studies) still has meaning for teachers and students.

7

Accountability and Reading Standards

"AGE OF ACCOUNTABILITY"

Throughout the first two hundred and fifty years of reading instruction in the United States, there have been many changes in the reasons and purposes for teaching reading, in the methods of teaching reading, and in the underlying philosophy for teaching reading.

Beginning in the last years of the twentieth century and moving into the first decade of the next, we are again witnessing another dramatic change, unlike anything we have seen in the past. One might be tempted to describe this new era as an "Age of Accountability."

It seems that at every level of education, from colleges of education to state boards of education, from local boards down to individual classroom teachers, the key to success is now dependent on meeting standards and being accountable for results. The Hawaii Department of Education (2005, p. 1) put it very succinctly: "Everyone in the Department of Education—teachers, principals, administrators, and support staff—will be held to high, measurable standards, and be responsible for achieving those standards." The momentum toward establishing national standards and calling for greater accountability began as far back as 1983 when the National Commission on Excellence in Education issued a report, *A Nation at Risk,* which warned against "a rising tide of mediocrity" in our schools. The results of this report spawned several educational changes. Instructional time in the classroom was increased, and time and efforts were spent on improving education at the local level.

A major shortcoming of this effort, however, was that it was too general in nature and lacked focus on academic standards. As the state superintendent of California later pointed out, "The desire to improve student achievement guided the effort, but it lacked a comprehensive, specific vision of what students actually need to know and be able to do" (Larsen & Eastin, 1997, p. 4).

Nine years later, the rising tide of mediocrity had not abated. In 1992, the National Assessment Governing Board in conjunction with the National Center for Educational Statistics tested more than twenty-six thousand Americans above the age of sixteen. The questions had to do with practical matters that face people every day, such as making out deposit slips and understanding instructions given to jurors. Careful demographic samplings were made that included accurate portions of males and females from all ethnic and racial groups from a variety of geographic locations.

The results were alarming, as only 3 percent read at the advanced level. Extrapolating from the results of the adult testing, the researchers, in their report entitled *Adult Literacy in America*, concluded that there are approximately *forty-two million functionally illiterate adults in this country*, and many millions more who were near illiterate (U.S. Department of Education, 1993). Regarding that same study, The *New York Times* on September 9, 1993, published a front-page article titled "Study Shows That Half of the Adults in U.S. Can't Read or Handle Arithmetic." It went on to report that businesses lose between twenty-five to thirty billion dollars as a result of errors and accidents attributed to poor literacy.

Somewhat along the same line, in 1996 the *National Assessment of Educational Progress* (NAEP), which provides the only ongoing survey of students' educational progress, issued the following findings for the nation, regions, and states:

- The average reading proficiency of twelfth graders declined significantly from 1992 to 1994. This decline was observed across a broad range of subgroups. Significant changes in average proficiency were not observed in the national population of fourth and eighth graders.
- The percentage of twelfth-grade students who reached the Proficient level in reading declined from 1992 to 1994. There was also a decline in the percentage of twelfth graders at or above the Basic level.
- In 1994, 30 percent of fourth graders, 30 percent of eighth graders, and 36 percent of twelfth graders attained the Proficient level in reading. Across the three grades, 3 to 7 percent reached the Advanced level.
- The decline in overall reading proficiency at the twelfth grade was evident in all three assessed purposes for reading: reading for literary experience, reading to gain information, and reading to perform a task.
- In 1994, fourth-, eighth-, and twelfth-grade students attending nonpublic schools displayed higher average reading proficiencies than did their counterparts attending public schools. (U.S. Department of Education, 1996)

NO CHILD LEFT BEHIND
AND READING FIRST LEGISLATION

Realizing that something drastic had to be done to increase reading ability, especially for children from low-income families and, based on the findings of the National Reading Panel (NRP), President George W. Bush proposed a sweeping new initiative called No Child Left Behind (NCLB) during his very first week in office. A year later (2002) the Act was passed into law with the strong endorsement and support from members of both parties of Congress. This legislation also established a national reading program called Reading First, which provides funds to support local efforts to enhance the early language, literacy, and reading development of preschool and primary-aged students, especially those from low-income families (U.S. Department of Education, 2005).

This act contains the president's four basic education reform principles:

- Stronger accountability for results
- Increased flexibility and local control
- Expanded options for teachers
- Emphasis on teaching methods that have proven to work (Block & Israel, 2005)

NCLB and Reading First legislation set into motion a whole string of events affecting not only how reading should be taught, but also how education would be evaluated. The new age of accountability was given birth.

EARLY READING FIRST AND
READING FIRST PROGRAMS

Although both federal initiatives—Early Reading First and Reading First—bear the same last two names, it is important that we don't confuse the two. Early Reading First is focused on nationwide efforts to enable or prepare children to read. Reading First is directed toward children in the early primary grades to ensure they receive proper instruction in classrooms.

Early Reading First

Early Reading First is directed primarily toward preschool children of low-income families to ensure that they receive instruction and activities to lay the foundation for good reading habits. This first phase of the reading program was set up with the hope and expectation that getting off to a good start in reading was paramount. The U.S. Department of Education (2004) concluded that, "With proper and systematic opportunities to develop fundamental skills during early childhood, as few as 5 percent of children may suffer serious reading difficulties."

Specifically, Early Reading First provides funds to:

- Support local efforts to enhance early language, cognitive, and reading developmental skills based on scientific research.
- Create high-quality language- and print-rich environments.
- Engage in scientifically based activities that promote the development of language, phonological awareness, print awareness, and alphabet knowledge.
- Identify preschool-age children who are at risk for reading failure.
- Integrate scientifically based instructional materials and programs into existing preschool programs.

Reading First

Reading First is part of NCLB and provides more than a billion dollars a year to help children learn to read. Reading First is dedicated to ensuring that all students learn to read on grade level by grade three. It provides money to states and school districts to encourage and support high-quality reading programs based on proven research.

Reading First is not a federally mandated program as some educators suggest. School districts are free not to participate if they so choose. Nor is it a one-size-fits-all kind of program. Those school districts that apply and receive grants may set up their programs to fit their particular needs with the one condition that programs be based on the latest and most available scientific research. Funds are available to school districts in which students are systematically and explicitly taught the following five skills as defined in the Report of the National Reading Panel (2000):

- Phonemic awareness: the ability to hear and identify sounds in spoken words
- Phonics: the relationship between the letters of written language and the sounds of spoken language
- Fluency: the capacity to read text accurately and quickly
- Vocabulary: the words that students must know to communicate effectively
- Comprehension: the ability to understand and gain meaning from what has been read

There are other components of Reading First. The program funds professional development, materials and strategies, valid and reliable screening, diagnostic and ongoing classroom assessments, and statewide accountability and leadership structures.

As a direct result of Reading First grants, nearly one hundred thousand teachers across the country from kindergarten through grade three have been trained to implement high-quality, scientifically based reading programs. Their efforts are reaching more than 1.5 million children.

As part of the accountability provisions of NCLB, every state has established grade-level standards for reading achievement with the objective that every child will meet state-defined standards by the end of

2013–2014. To reach that objective each state has developed benchmarks (or goals) to measure progress and make sure that every student is meeting those objectives. State Departments of Education are required by law to evaluate individual school districts' data and holding schools accountable for subgroups of students so that no child falls through the cracks. School districts that do not meet "Adequate Yearly Progress" (AYP) are considered "in need of improvement" (U.S. Department of Education, n.d., p. 4).

Since these standards are so comprehensive and specific and vary from state to state, we refer readers to Resource A (Texas Reading Standards for Elementary Grades) and Resource B (The Continuum Approach) for a more detailed explanation.

NCLB standards have had a dramatic effect on all segments of the educational world. They have great impact on the reading curriculum and methods of teaching reading for state boards of education, local school districts, individual teachers, and parents themselves.

Impact on State Boards of Education

Under the accountability provisions of NCLB, states must describe how they will close the achievement gap and make sure that all students, especially those who are disadvantaged, achieve academic proficiency. They must produce annual state and school district report cards that inform parents and the community about state and school progress.

The boards of education in all fifty states have now established state standards for teaching reading and other subjects that apply to all grade levels, kindergarten through 12, based upon the recommendation of the National Reading Council. These grade-level goals spell out, or enumerate, specific goals that are to be met at each level. (As mentioned above, in Resource Section A, you will find an example of one state's grade-level expectations for phonemic awareness and phonics instruction.)

Impact on Local School Districts

Following the lead of the state boards of education, each individual school district is expected to follow the state guidelines (or standards) for meeting reading goals at each level.

To evaluate whether or not children were reaching grade-level expectations, NCLB required that beginning in the 2002–2003 school year all schools had to administer tests in each grade span: grades 3–5, grades 6–9, and grades 10–12. Beginning in 2005–2006, tests must be administered in grades 3–8 in math and reading. Beginning in the 2007–2008 school year, science achievement must also be tested.

School districts must submit an annual report to the state showing that they are making Adequate Yearly Progress (AYP).

Schools that do not make progress must provide supplemental programs, such as free tutoring or afterschool assistance. If children do not make adequate yearly progress after five years, there must be major adjustments to the way in which the school is run.

Awards will be granted to school districts and individual schools that make major gains in achievement.

Impact on Teachers

NCLB and the findings of the NRP have had the most effect on classroom teachers who are the recipients of all the state and national mandates.

Now the total responsibility for making programs work and children achieve falls squarely on the shoulders of individual teachers. Today the teachers must not only know the subjects that they are teaching well, but must also be responsible for increases in learning, results for which are sometimes beyond their control. The teacher must have one eye on the subject and the other eye on evaluation.

Starting in the 2005–2006 year, teachers must have at least a bachelor's degree, be fully certified as defined by the state board of education, and be able to demonstrate subject-area competence in any core subject taught.

IS NCLB WORKING?

Since the start of NCLB in 2002, the big question that those involved in education were asking was: "Does the Program Work?" Taxpayers were wondering: "Are we getting our money's worth, or is this just another boondoggle?"

For over thirty years, the NAEP had been using the same tests for reading and math to find out how well our students were progressing in those subject areas. These reports, also known as the "Nation's Report Card," showed that from 1971, when they first started gathering data, until 1999 the fluctuations of scores were incremental in nature and generally in a downward trend (National Center for Educational Statistics, 2003).

Unlike with federal initiatives of the past, it didn't take long before educators and legislators had good evidence that all their planning and efforts on behalf of NCLB were working and improvement was evident on many different levels.

For the years 1999 through 2006, they began to witness amazing positive results in reading and math. Reports on reading scores only are reported below. (Starting as far back as 1999, several states, such as Texas, California, and Virginia, had already established statewide grade-level objectives to be met by all school districts in each of those states. Results in reading improvement from those states were positive. Due to the good results that then-Governor Bush had with his program in Texas, the notion of No Child Left Behind was established nationwide. The improvement in reading in these states led directly to NCLB.)

The long-term Nation's Report Card results (NAEP, 2005), for example, reported that elementary school student achievement in reading and math were at all-time highs and that the achievement gap between minorities and the majority was closing. It showed:

- There was more progress for nine-year-olds in reading over the past five years than in the previous twenty-eight years combined.
- Nine-year-old students posted the best scores in reading since 1973 and in math since 1973. These nine-year-olds received the highest math scores that the tests have ever recorded.
- Reading scores for nine-year-old African American and Hispanic students reached an all-time high.
- Achievement gaps in reading and math between nine-year-old African American and Hispanic students are at an all-time low.
- In state-by-state reporting, forty-three states and the District of Columbia either improved academically or held steady in all categories for fourth- and eighth-grade reading and math.
- Reports regarding urban education showed that students in select urban school districts improved faster than their peers over the past two years.
- Between 2002 and 2005, urban fourth graders posted a 14 percent-point gain in math and an eleven percent-point gain in reading. (U.S. Department of Education, 2006)

CONCLUSION

It is remarkable how the demand for educational accountability and more educational standards has evolved in the last few decades. In 1990, for example, very few states worked at setting educational standards. By 2003, however, all fifty states had already passed or were in the process of developing academic standards for all students at all grade levels.

At about the same time, more and more teachers, parents, administrators, and professional organizations were asking for clearer and more research-based guidelines with which to frame educational objectives. Specifically, teachers and parents want to know what is expected at each grade level.

Integrating phonics topics into the reading standards helps ensure that students receive systematic, explicit phonics instruction as part of their reading program. Clear, specific reading standards that include phonics help parents and teachers answer questions such as: How do phonics skills build on each other? How can they best be taught, and how can we evaluate them? What kind of intervention program do we need, and how early should it start? What do we do when children don't meet these standards? Like the other reading instruction approaches with which it should be integrated, phonics requires goals or standards to give it meaning and direction. Setting phonics standards also serves to clarify the subject, provide a set of expectations, and elevate expectations (Kendall & Marzano, 1997).

While well-crafted state and national standards are a great potential help to all teachers and parents, let us remember that good teachers have always had high standards, for both themselves and the students they teach. Standards, whether state mandated or self-imposed, have always been a critical part of an effective reading program in the past and will continue to be in the years to come.

Informal
Reading Tests

Evaluation of students' progress in reading is an ongoing process. Teachers can learn a great deal about individuals' strong points and weak points by simply listening as each student reads, and then they can make notes of the types of mistakes the student makes—noting whether these are mostly substitution mistakes or mistakes resulting from poor phonics skills. Teachers also rely heavily on the unit tests, which are generally given at the completion of a block of material, and standardized tests, which are generally administered at the end of the school year to assess progress, or lack thereof, in reading.

While these unit and standardized tests can be meaningful and helpful in diagnosing areas of strength and weakness, they have their limitations. Standardized tests are generally administered one or two times a year, usually at the end of a semester or year. Standardized tests tend to be more national in scope and also lean toward placing children into categories—average, above average, and below average. Standardized tests do a better job of comparing "achievement with the achievement of other students at the local, state, or national levels" (Burns, 2006, p. 237). These tests may not reflect what has been taught in the classroom. Teachers more and more are moving away from reliance on standardized and commercially produced tests and are making more use of informal classroom assessment (Strickland, 1998).

ABOUT THE TESTS

Informal or teacher-made tests, such as those presented in this chapter, are more clearly directed at material recently taught—the alphabet, consonants, syllabication, etc. They are meant to measure the progress of one group or one student and have validity only for that group. These tests are usually given right, or shortly, after teachers have presented material or spent time on a particular aspect of reading. Teachers make up their own tests and administer them to an individual or group of students. In correcting the tests, they receive immediate feedback on students' skill levels and can plan upcoming lessons accordingly. Informal tests are generally short and to the point and meant for diagnostic purposes only. They are handy things to show parents at parent-teacher conferences to illustrate a given student's level of mastery or the student's particular needs.

The tests in this chapter are illustrative of the types of informal tests teachers construct and use when assessing phonics progress. These tests are not exhaustive. Teachers might choose to use some of the tests as is or treat them as examples in creating their own informal tests. Most of the tests are very broad and could be administered at different grade levels. They are the kind of assessment teachers might use after students have taken a series of smaller tests. For example, a first grade teacher could use parts of the test on consonants, but unless her students are quite advanced, she should not expect them to do well on the entire test. A third grade teacher, on the other hand, could administer the test to the entire class and expect most of them to do well. An upper elementary teacher might use some of the tests presented here to get a better idea of what a student, or group of students, still needs in the way of phonics instruction.

The tests in this chapter are not intended for grade marks (e.g., A, B, D)—unit tests or standardized tests are better suited for that purpose. The tests presented here are meant to be indicators of what a student knows in a specific area and should be used for the continued assessment needed in all reading programs.

ADMINISTERING THE TESTS

Even though these are informal tests, it is very important that the teacher explain to the student or group why the test is being administered, why it is important that they try their best, and how much time is allotted for the test. The students should be allowed to ask any questions before the test begins. During the test the teacher should not give any help or instructions, other than procedural clarifications. The teacher should instruct the students not to spend too much time on one answer. Tell the students to go on to the next item and come back to the items they did not answer on the first pass.

SCORING THE TESTS

These tests are not scored with a letter grade; they are indicators of whether a student has mastered a particular skill or not. A perfect or near-perfect score means mastery at least at the time of the test. Any student who misses more than twenty-five percent of the items obviously needs additional practice and review. Teachers should keep records of how students do on the tests for future reference. Keeping track of individual students' progress in phonics topics is important, since lack of knowledge in one or more of these areas is a good indicator of present and future problems.

COMMENTS ON INDIVIDUAL TESTS

Below are comments on each test in this chapter. They provide information such as the grade levels for which the test is appropriate and notes on administering the test. It is recommended that teachers read the comments before deciding whether to give a test to their students.

The Manuscript Alphabet (K–2)

[Figure 8.1] The test for the manuscript alphabet should be given to students in kindergarten through second grade. All letters, both uppercase and lowercase, should be written in exact alphabetical order. The time limit should not exceed ten minutes.

The Cursive Alphabet (Grade 3 and Above)

[Figure 8.2] All students in third grade or above should be able to write all the letters of the alphabet in upper- and lowercase in both manuscript and cursive handwriting in exact alphabetical order. For third graders and upper elementary students it is important that both alphabets be presented together in order to make sure students know both forms and are not substituting manuscript letters for cursive letters and vice versa.

Foundation Words I (Grade 2 and Above)

[Figure 8.3] This test asks students to distinguish words from non-words and requires a certain degree of both word recognition and decoding skills. The words that are correctly spelled are all within the listening and reading vocabularies of elementary students and are generally found in the reading material of this age group. Teachers may want to substitute words students have recently studied for those in this test.

Foundation Words II (Grade 3 and Above)

[Figure 8.4] This test is similar to the previous one except that the words represent a slightly greater degree of difficulty. This test can be modified to include words recently studied in reading class. Unmodified, it may be given to students in the third grade or above to get an indication of their word-recognition skills.

Beginning and Ending Consonants (Grades 1 and 2)

[Figures 8.5 & 8.6, with answer keys below] The test on initial consonant sounds is appropriate for students at the end of first grade who have had a lot of practice with beginning sounds. The ending sounds could be saved for the middle of second grade. It is important that the teachers pronounce each word clearly with emphasis on the beginning sounds for the first test and on the ending sounds for the second. They should repeat the clue word twice and not go back to repeat words later on.

[Figure 8.5] Beginning Sounds answers:

1. game	11. jet
2. kick	12. vase
3. so	13. gem
4. pan	14. mice
5. quack	15. yell
6. love	16. paint
7. fish	17. will
8. hat	18. ride
9. zip	19. boat
10. keep	20. camp

[Figure 8.6] Ending Sounds answers:

1. luck	11. jar
2. whiz	12. golf
3. corn	13. cut
4. mob	14. jeep
5. six	15. bad
6. fail	16. dress
7. bug	17. her
8. love	18. picnic
9. try	19. word
10. ham	20. which

Common Endings (Grade 2 and Above)

[Figure 8.7] This test is quite long and inclusive. It tests knowledge of some of the most important ending sounds, or phonograms, students are likely to encounter in early reading material. This test is appropriate only if students have had sufficient prior experience with phonograms. The teacher may want to break this test into a series of shorter ones. This is also a good test for identification of initial consonants.

Contractions (Grade 4 and Above)

[Figure 8.8] Although students meet contractions early on in reading, the test below presupposes that students have been exposed in some way to all the contractions and that they have had practice writing them. For this reason it is better to postpone this comprehensive type of test until fourth grade or later. This test also makes a good review for students in the junior high or middle school grades who often confuse certain forms.

Initial Consonant Blends and Digraphs (Grade 3 and Above)

[Figure 8.9] This test represents a more comprehensive type, including thirty-seven double and triple blends and digraphs. Before students are exposed to this test they should have had less inclusive informal testing at earlier grade levels. This test could be very useful for teachers in the upper grades who have students with serious reading problems.

Forming Plurals (Grade 4 and Above)

[Figure 8.10] Students become exposed to plural endings at a very early stage of reading. In the first few grades it is necessary to explain what plurals are and how to form them as they come up in reading. The test in this chapter is rather comprehensive and involves a great many spelling changes and ideas that are not presented until the fourth and fifth grades, and beyond. Many older students and even adults might have difficulty with some of the items on this test.

Vowel Sounds (Grade 2 and Above)

[Figure 8.11] Sections of this test, especially words with short vowels, can be handled by most second graders. Some of the vowel digraphs that represent long vowel sounds may be difficult for third graders. Continuous testing of vowel sounds is necessary not only because vowels are such a challenging aspect of learning to read, but also because success in unit and standardized tests is often contingent on the students' knowledge of vowel sounds.

Dividing Words Into Syllables (Grade 3 and Above)

[Figure 8.12] In this particular test it is not all that important that the students divide every word correctly as long as they keep the vowel sounds apart and remove prefixes and suffixes. For example, dividing woman as wo-man or level as le-vel would be acceptable. On the other hand, such spellings as goo-dness would not be acceptable since the student in this case obviously does not know how to pronounce the word. Some teacher judgment is necessary in correcting this test.

Prefixes and Suffixes (Grade 3 and Above)

[Figures 8.13a & 8.13b] Although most phonics lessons are completed by the end of third grade or early in fourth grade, prefixes, suffixes, and root words are taught extensively from third grade on. In later elementary grades, junior high, and high school, teachers take time to further develop knowledge of root words and affixes. The prefixes and suffixes in this test should be easily identifiable by most third and fourth graders.

Word Checklists (Grade 1 and Above)

[Figures 8.14a–8.14c, 8.15a–8.15c, 8.16a–8.16c] Each Word Checklist test consists of two hundred words selected from reading lists and student classroom texts. Word Checklist I is for first and second graders. The words in this test were randomly selected from various reading lists and books that students use in beginning reading classes. By the end of first grade or the beginning of second grade, students should be able to recognize these words with little hesitation. Word Checklist II is for grade two and above. The words in this test were randomly selected from material that second and third graders often encounter in the process of developing reading skills. The words should be easily recognizable by average and above-average students at this level. Students having reading problems in the upper elementary grades might also profit from going through this list. Word Checklist III is for grade four and above. The words are a random selection of important concept words that often appear in science, mathematics, and geography textbooks and materials used in the later elementary grades. Both pronunciation and understanding of these words are important. Note that the polysyllabic words in these checklists can also be used to test students' skills in dividing words into syllables.

Administering the Word Checklist Tests: This is a one-on-one test. Do one column at a time. Ask individual students to read each word on the list. If anyone is hesitant, ask the student to try to sound out the word. Any student not able to say the word should go on to the next word. On your copy of the test, put a check on the line next to the missed word. Record the number of misses at the bottom of the column. After the the list is completed, the teacher may try to help figure out why certain words were missed and give a few clues to help the next time the student encounters those words. If the student has a perfect or near-perfect score, go on to the next column. Do not attempt to complete all the columns in one sitting, unless the student is willing and able. The next time you go over the list with the student, begin with the missed words first and proceed from there.

The Manuscript Alphabet

Name_____ Date_____

Directions: Write all the missing letters of the alphabet in proper alphabetical order. You must include both capital and small letters.

Aa _____ Cc _____ _____ Ff

_____ Hh _____ _____ _____ Ll

_____ _____ Oo _____ _____ _____

_____ Tt _____ Vv _____ _____

_____ Zz

Figure 8.1

The Cursive Alphabet

Name_____ Date_____

Directions: Write all the missing letters of the alphabet in proper alphabetical order. You must include both capital and small letters.

_____ _____ *Cc* _____ _____ _____

Gg _____ _____ _____ *Kk* _____

_____ _____ *Oo* _____ _____ _____

Ss _____ _____ *Vv* _____ _____

_____ _____

Figure 8.2

Foundation Words I

Name_____ Date_____

Directions: Circle two words in each line that are not really words.

1. clean	funy	play	with	cume	do
2. dish	four	fathur	left	sume	too
3. box	aet	kind	rhuse	sat	house
4. skool	olde	let	jump	over	three
5. time	wish	toye	tuke	zoo	blew
6. shall	agin	wuz	them	seven	five
7. boke	babby	food	girl	now	new
8. onlly	off	seid	party	it's	how
9. live	morning	late	grean	great	ouce
10. saw	ferst	thin	first	whair	here
11. do	lind	around	next	tall	wer
12. good	without	who	stope	you	peeple

Figure 8.3

Foundation Words II

Name_____ Date_____

Directions: Circle two words in each line that are not really words.

1. cowboy	beginning	curcus	child	wate	either
2. voise	table	streat	state	store	seed
3. buy	corn	beet	creem	treat	peece
4. caben	below	water	pitchur	sunny	prize
5. cried	knew	budd	chen	teeth	truth
6. stor	ground	reach	rake	report	retern
7. smell	smill	smull	small	smile	smells
8. sity	block	being	rabit	child	children
9. ring	rang	rung	rong	ringe	wrote
10. womin	piece	window	won	weer	wore
11. hemself	plant	rain	enside	animal	bear
12. eight	right	sister	pleeze	brow	puch

Figure 8.4

Beginning Consonants

Name_____ Date_____

Directions: Listen carefully as your teacher pronounces each word. Pay particular attention to the beginning sound of each word. Complete the word by writing the letter or letters that represent the sound you hear.

1. ____ame   11. ____et

2. ____ick   12. ____ase

3. ____o   13. ____em

4. ____an   14. ____ice

5. ____ack   15. ____ell

6. ____ove   16. ____aint

7. ____ish   17. ____ill

8. ____at   18. ____ide

9. ____ip   19. ____oat

10. ____eep   20. ____amp

Figure 8.5

Ending Consonants

Name_____ Date_____

Directions: Listen carefully as your teacher pronounces each word. Pay particular attention to the sound you hear at the end of each word. Complete the word by writing the letter or letters that represent the sound you hear.

1. luc____   11. ja____

2. whi____   12. gol____

3. cor____   13. cu____

4. mo____   14. jee____

5. si____   15. ba____

6. fai____   16. dres____

7. bu____   17. he____

8. lo____e   18. picni____

9. tr____   19. wor____

10. ha____   20. whic____

Figure 8.6

Common Endings

Name_____ Date_____

Directions: Write a consonant letter on the line to make a word.

1. ____at	14. ____in	27. ____ink
2. ____ut	15. ____ell	28. ____ear
3. ____ill	16. ____ug	29. ____one
4. ____ent	17. ____ace	30. ____end
5. ____ap	18. ____ess	31. ____ine
6. ____ew	19. ____all	32. ____est
7. ____ot	20. ____ing	33. ____ock
8. ____it	21. ____eed	34. ____ar
9. ____ay	22. ____ang	35. ____op
10. ____ow	23. ____uck	36. ____ipe
11. ____ip	24. ____ad	37. ____ite
12. ____eat	25. ____ight	38. ____ump
13. ____od	26. ____ane	

Figure 8.7

Contractions

Name_____ Date_____

Directions: Write the correct contraction next to the two words.

1. are not_____

2. could not_____

3. does not_____

4. had not_____

5. have not_____

6. should not_____

7. were not_____

8. would not_____

9. you are_____

10. they are_____

11. I will_____

12. she will_____

13. you will_____

14. it will_____

15. I have_____

16. you have_____

17. he has_____

18. that is_____

Directions: Write two words that have the same meaning as the contractions.

1. can't_____

2. didn't_____

3. doesn't_____

4. hasn't_____

5. isn't_____

6. we'll_____

7. they'll_____

8. that'll_____

9. we've_____

10. they've_____

11. wasn't_____

12. won't_____

13. we're_____

14. they're_____

15. he'll_____

16. she's_____

17. it's_____

18. there's_____

Figure 8.8

Initial Consonant Blends and Digraphs

Name_____ Date_____

Directions: Choose an ending that goes with the blend sound to make a word. Draw a circle around that ending. The first one is done for you.

1. bl	-ace	(-ow)	-urch	-ooth		20. sp	-inch	-ench	-urch	-ine
2. cl	-ild	-oo	-imb	-ow		21. tr	-ock	-ibe	-ung	-ong
3. br	-imp	-ace	-urch	-ooth		22. sc	-ope	-ipe	-ump	-ime
4. ch	-itch	-ild	-oop	-imb		23. th	-im	-ip	-ope	-ink
5. sm	-ice	-inch	-ink	-art		24. tr	-est	-ack	-er	-ost
6. th	-ile	-ale	-in	-arp		25. fr	-im	-est	-ime	-esh
7. sw	-ink	-aw	-ice	-ell		26. gr	-ip	-ooth	-ine	-ild
8. st	-um	-art	-ap	-uce		27. sw	-ink	-eat	-ire	-ime
9. pl	-oop	-ar	-irp	-um		28. ch	-im	-ope	-ime	-urt
10. wh	-ile	-ep	-atch	ope		29. tw	-ime	-eet	-ore	-ure
11. sk	-unk	-ink	-enk	-onk		30. scr	-ap	-oat	-ash	-aye
12. fl	-ass	-ive	-ag	-ig		31. str	-irt	-urt	-art	-ay
13. cr	-oom	-iff	-ong	-ime		32. spr	-ipe	-ape	-ing	-ide
14. sh	-iff	-ench	-ow	-oop		33. thr	-ang	-ill	-uze	-ise
15. pr	-unt	-ench	-ong	-oom		34. shr	-use	-ide	-uce	-ed
16. sn	-ow	-im	-ing	-irt		35. spl	-ish	-ash	-ush	-ide
17. sk	-y	-ick	-urch	-ow		36. spr	-oate	-uss	-ay	-illy
18. gl	-ive	-ave	-ide	-uve		37. squ	-uce	-ide	-ate	-are
19. sl	-ench	-urch	-ice	-uce						

Figure 8.9

Forming Plurals

Name_____ Date_____

Directions: Change the singular nouns into plurals.

1. self_____

2. box_____

3. wife_____

4. berry_____

5. potato_____

6. radio_____

7. cracker_____

8. sheet_____

9. deer_____

10. life_____

11. forty_____

12. tax_____

13. ox_____

14. city_____

15. woman_____

16. sky_____

17. echo_____

18. dog_____

19. man_____

20. wolf_____

21. loss_____

22. church_____

23. sheep_____

24. money_____

25. pot_____

26. alumnus_____

27. hat_____

28. table_____

29. loaf_____

30. zero_____

Figure 8.10

Vowel Sounds

Name_____ Date_____

Directions: Underline all words with a long vowel sound. Circle all words with a short vowel sound.

1. got   2. time   3. see   4. not   5. go

6. lay   7. bat   8. when   9. look   10. lump

11. dog   12. mud   13. sent   14. blew   15. use

16. pot   17. eat   18. list   19. grade   20. by

Directions: Add a vowel (a, e, i, o, u , y) to make a word.

1. d____   2. nev__r   3. littl__   4. h__ke   5. __pen

6. b__at   7. h__pe   8. he__r   9. sev__n   10. f__me

11. st__te   12. lo__k   13. __s   14. fl__g   15. fac__

16. k__nd   17. __nder   18. w__rk   19. m__n   20. j__mp

Figure 8.11

Dividing Words Into Syllables

Name_____   Date_____

Directions: Divide the words into syllables.

1. letter_____

2. woman_____

3. cowboy_____

4. level_____

5. tulip_____

6. butterfly_____

7. pony_____

8. every_____

9. mistake_____

10. cabin_____

11. Internet_____

12. gentle_____

13. never_____

14. crazy_____

15. basket_____

16. runner_____

17. motor_____

18. poodle_____

19. color_____

20. afternoon_____

21. thanksgiving_____

22. goodness_____

23. understanding_____

24. forgetful_____

25. reward_____

26. locality_____

27. teacher_____

28. exactly_____

29. English_____

30. rumble_____

Figure 8.12

Prefixes and Suffixes

Name_____ Date_____

Directions: Circle the ending that goes with the prefix to make a new word. The first one is done for you.

1. pro	-spell	(-noun)	-tall	-meter	16. sub	-zip	-long	-tract	-lop
2. ex	-port	-stub	-part	-do	17. un	-load	-fere	-meter	-err
3. mis	-add	-lace	-gone	-place	18. mid	-going	-gone	-day	-fitting
4. ad	-spent	-mit	-angle	-fort	19. bi	-house	-dun	-cycle	-van
5. con	-sence	-cycle	-sent	-arm	20. de	-joy	-fax	-flirt	-part
6. re	-heat	-hot	-hut	-hurm	21. im	-sect	-cid	-polite	-pock
7. dis	-stop	-arm	-stair	-ploy	22. per	-mit	-ferm	-fort	-ture
8. fore	-mission	-tion	-arm	-dew	23. inter	-polite	-foll	-fere	-site
9. non	-stop	-tion	-shun	-mitty	24. in	-fire	-side	-hold	-pit
10. pre	-any	-brang	-blue	-pay	25. trans	-motion	-part	-joy	-mit
11. super	-dex	-mit	-star	-min	26. bi	-sect	-sycle	-build	-felt
12. post	-star	-store	-ion	-war	27. centi	-ury	-meters	-gone	-pix
13. co	-stip	-strange	-stand	-star	28. tri	-ally	-angle	-angel	-fully
14. anti	-freeze	-gone	-loppe	-stair	29. dia	-happy	-meter	-ppurs	-locks
15. per	-handel	-form	-do	-hops	30. over	-chur	-do	-ploy	-side

Figure 8.13a

Prefixes and Suffixes

Name_____ Date_____

Directions: Add one of the following endings (*-ed*, *-ing*, *-ful*, *-ly*, *-ive*, *-y*, *-ment*, *-en*, *-less*, *-ness*, *-tion*, *-sion*) to the spaces below to make words.

1. act_____   11. snow_____

2. hitt_____   12. dark_____

3. vi_____   13. funn_____

4. state_____   14. pass_____

5. need_____   15. good_____

6. vaca_____   16. happi_____

7. jell_____   17. less_____

8. quick_____   18. talk_____

9. color_____   19. froz_____

10. poor_____   20. ill_____

Figure 8.13b

Word Checklist I

Name_____ Date_____

Directions: Read each word aloud.

___ in	___ to	___ me	___ up
___ it	___ all	___ I	___ very
___ a	___ will	___ good	___ there
___ and	___ on	___ so	___ when
___ be	___ has	___ day	___ by
___ can	___ that	___ had	___ the
___ as	___ big	___ from	___ come
___ have	___ this	___ if	___ get
___ at	___ second	___ he	___ go
___ for	___ with	___ one	___ him
___ **Score**	___ **Score**	___ **Score**	___ **Score**

___ an	___ do	___ say	___ also
___ call	___ bat	___ saw	___ bit
___ words	___ first	___ use	___ soon
___ thing	___ than	___ after	___ home
___ tell	___ way	___ these	___ into
___ children	___ think	___ apple	___ house
___ which	___ found	___ eat	___ made
___ water	___ she	___ cap	___ her
___ you	___ away	___ four	___ over
___ find	___ where	___ time	___ same
___ **Score**	___ **Score**	___ **Score**	___ **Score**

Figure 8.14a

Word Checklist I

Name_____   Date_____

Directions: Read each word aloud.

____ them	____ give	____ back	____ just
____ what	____ here	____ but	____ short
____ came	____ five	____ old	____ three
____ put	____ each	____ again	____ said
____ two	____ cat	____ write	____ before
____ could	____ after	____ new	____ work
____ other	____ because	____ find	____ school
____ under	____ more	____ jump	____ ago
____ few	____ wait	____ night	____ well
____ into	____ soon	____ until	____ stand
____ **Score**	____ **Score**	____ **Score**	____ **Score**

____ began	____ sun	____ like	____ of
____ they	____ eleven	____ make	____ about
____ went	____ air	____ little	____ some
____ draw	____ my	____ many	____ his
____ ride	____ next	____ how	____ to
____ ask	____ too	____ no	____ we
____ send	____ another	____ now	____ was
____ red	____ dear	____ or	____ out
____ fall	____ is	____ see	____ take
____ land	____ know	____ they	____ us
____ **Score**	____ **Score**	____ **Score**	____ **Score**

Figure 8.14b

Word Checklist I

Name_____ Date_____

Directions: Read each word aloud.

___ car	___ moon	___ find	___ were
___ begun	___ tree	___ more	___ long
___ still	___ been	___ it's	___ then
___ sing	___ dog	___ hat	___ their
___ not	___ tall	___ around	___ down
___ ten	___ white	___ hit	___ which
___ may	___ upon	___ look	___ am
___ six	___ say	___ not	___ ever
___ every	___ seem	___ much	___ day
___ hide	___ sure	___ let	___ orange
___ **Score**	___ **Score**	___ **Score**	___ **Score**

Figure 8.14c

Word Checklist II (Grade 2 and Above)

Name_____ Date_____

Directions: Read each word aloud.

___ wash	___ inside	___ heart	___ hurt
___ food	___ circus	___ nothing	___ inside
___ everyone	___ dark	___ miss	___ wind
___ cry	___ need	___ beside	___ six
___ cake	___ catch	___ milk	___ wet
___ bed	___ feel	___ himself	___ mom
___ glad	___ face	___ plant	___ cage
___ drink	___ mean	___ sky	___ true
___ bill	___ never	___ fine	___ winter
___ box	___ side	___ sing	___ stay
___ **Score**	___ **Score**	___ **Score**	___ **Score**

___ please	___ pretty	___ myself	___ river
___ young	___ being	___ country	___ start
___ bright	___ head	___ learn	___ street
___ brother	___ family	___ zoo	___ ready
___ pick	___ across	___ once	___ sea
___ blow	___ sentence	___ brown	___ rest
___ party	___ morning	___ boat	___ space
___ hide	___ present	___ someone	___ really
___ kept	___ pie	___ cookies	___ care
___ belong	___ sometimes	___ happy	___ tiny
___ **Score**	___ **Score**	___ **Score**	___ **Score**

Figure 8.15a

Word Checklist II

Name_____ Date_____

Directions: Read each word aloud.

___ against	___ lived	___ store	___ pig
___ game	___ maybe	___ seven	___ roll
___ found	___ leg	___ jet	___ kill
___ enough	___ room	___ tail	___ throw
___ ground	___ out	___ else	___ lady
___ hole	___ cloud	___ dress	___ dip
___ heard	___ remember	___ strong	___ sink
___ dirt	___ ship	___ king	___ jar
___ happen	___ show	___ desk	___ tin
___ glass	___ tall	___ flow	___ began
___ **Score**	___ **Score**	___ **Score**	___ **Score**
___ down	___ bear	___ pull	___ right
___ band	___ wire	___ police	___ ear
___ dad	___ drill	___ war	___ lost
___ people	___ bake	___ dock	___ fit
___ fell	___ butter	___ carpet	___ tonight
___ bag	___ answer	___ flat	___ within
___ gone	___ win	___ fat	___ nest
___ wall	___ frog	___ lamp	___ dust
___ drip	___ cart	___ coat	___ grandma
___ swim	___ held	___ easy	___ pin
___ **Score**	___ **Score**	___ **Score**	___ **Score**

Figure 8.15b

Word Checklist II

Name_____ Date_____

Directions: Read each word aloud.

___ wheel	___ bench	___ dance	___ drank
___ voice	___ junk	___ drove	___ bark
___ chew	___ bath	___ bold	___ candy
___ oh	___ drunk	___ cash	___ knock
___ true	___ cream	___ birth	___ chair
___ clip	___ stay	___ useless	___ grass
___ knife	___ flag	___ birthday	___ penny
___ deep	___ happy	___ enter	___ blow
___ village	___ sock	___ whole	___ anyone
___ tap	___ foot	___ chop	___ doctor
___ **Score**	___ **Score**	___ **Score**	___ **Score**

Figure 8.15c

Word Checklist III

Name_____ Date_____

Directions: Read each word aloud.

___ amount	___ temperature	___ triple	___ solve
___ infection	___ residence	___ international	___ column
___ fossil	___ centimeter	___ rectangle	___ location
___ laboratory	___ magazine	___ sample	___ length
___ receipt	___ gravity	___ credit	___ nurse
___ elevator	___ digit	___ weight	___ sequence
___ infection	___ count	___ movies	___ manual
___ newspaper	___ sharing	___ quart	___ gas
___ square	___ pulse	___ medicine	___ segment
___ zero	___ component	___ gram	___ principal
___ **Score**	___ **Score**	___ **Score**	___ **Score**

___ material	___ schedule	___ highway	___ plane
___ size	___ prime	___ positive	___ alarm
___ angle	___ secretary	___ sum	___ liter
___ marker	___ depth	___ connect	___ double
___ century	___ solution	___ survey	___ atom
___ difference	___ standard	___ radio	___ accident
___ ounce	___ outcome	___ vertical	___ balance
___ equator	___ inches	___ product	___ straight
___ building	___ emergency	___ rate	___ quality
___ satellite	___ magnet	___ produce	___ prescribe
___ **Score**	___ **Score**	___ **Score**	___ **Score**

Figure 8.16a

Word Checklist III

Name_____ Date_____

Directions: Read each word aloud.

____ minus	____ fraction	____ physical	____ opposite
____ data	____ depth	____ interest	____ reservation
____ extension	____ mineral	____ equation	____ horizontal
____ addend	____ nickel	____ least	____ odds
____ mathematics	____ microscope	____ pressure	____ volcano
____ parallel	____ pupil	____ equal	____ recognition
____ numerator	____ capacity	____ estimate	____ calendar
____ business	____ universal	____ extinct	____ denominator
____ taste	____ family	____ negative	____ pattern
____ scale	____ thousand	____ elastic	____ entrance
____ **Score**	____ **Score**	____ **Score**	____ **Score**

____ segment	____ density	____ insect	____ actual
____ positive	____ random	____ radiant	____ solid
____ surface	____ graph	____ cube	____ sphere
____ magnetic	____ even	____ transportation	____ nutrition
____ infinite	____ organ	____ distance	____ prediction
____ liberty	____ experiment	____ manufacture	____ timetable
____ northwest	____ skeleton	____ vitamin	____ instructor
____ liquid	____ colonial	____ digestion	____ colony
____ battery	____ partial	____ treatment	____ hunger
____ information	____ chemistry	____ billion	____ creation
____ **Score**	____ **Score**	____ **Score**	____ **Score**

Figure 8.16b

Word Checklist III (Grade 4 and Above)

Name_____ Date_____

Directions: Read each word aloud.

____ industry	____ direction	____ money	____ million
____ angle	____ quotient	____ fern	____ complex
____ electricity	____ mass	____ multiplication	____ policy
____ compound	____ telephone	____ middle	____ pollute
____ statistic	____ quantity	____ ratio	____ triangular
____ scissors	____ single	____ civilization	____ democracy
____ unequal	____ friction	____ whole	____ fuel
____ federal	____ revolutionary	____ operator	____ symbol
____ behavior	____ locality	____ simple	____ census
____ focus	____ similar	____ telegram	____ independence
____ **Score**	____ **Score**	____ **Score**	____ **Score**

Figure 8.16c

Resource A: Reading Standards for Elementary Grades

Before presenting a listing of grade-level standards, it is important to remember that every child in every classroom is unique, not only in size and shape, but in learning ability as well. Just because a child is in the first grade does not mean that he/she is learning only first grade material. Some children may have advanced reading skills and thus should get help at a more advanced level. Other students will need additional help with readiness tasks. The teacher should be prepared to help on all levels—advanced, average, or remedial.

Grade-level standards are more than just guides to what the child should be expected to know at that level. They are a means to keep the teacher and students on course and indicators for parents concerning what children are expected to know at each level. Most important, the standards mentioned in this section represent a renewal of public commitment to making improvements in the ways children are learning to read. The former superintendent of the state board of education in California goes one step further, stating that, "Standards are our [California's] commitment to excellence." She goes on to predict:

Fifteen years from now, we are convinced, the adoption of standards will be viewed as the single event that began "the rising tide of excellence" in our schools. No more will the critical question "What should my child be learning?" be met with uncertainty of knowledge, purpose and resolve. These [California] standards answer the question. They are comprehensive and specific. They represent our commitment to excellence. (California Department of Education)

Standards are goals. When goals are not met, it simply means that more time and effort should be devoted to that task.

Although all fifty state boards of education now have grade-level standards for reading, I have selected the Texas grade-level standards for review for a couple of reasons. They are explicit, complete, well stated, and in the public domain—which means they can be reproduced without permission. I feel that most state standards follow the same general lines as those of Texas.

It is important to point out that the statewide standards mentioned here represent only one view of the reading spectrum and should not be considered complete in any sense of the word. All teachers, especially those just entering the profession, are encouraged to read the complete standards for their state or school district. These standards can generally be obtained by writing the state board of education. Many of them can be found on the Internet.

For practical application of standards for teaching phonetic skills, teachers are directed to the Reading Skills Checklist in Resource C.

TEXAS READING STANDARDS FOR ELEMENTARY GRADES

Because of the length and inclusiveness of the Texas standards and the nature of this book, only those standards that have relevance to reading and to skills related directly to phonemic awareness and structural analysis of words are included below. Many reading standards such as those listed under "Listening Skills," "Comprehension," and "Language Arts Skills" were excluded, not because they are not considered important, but because they didn't fall within the purview of this book. Excluded also were statewide standards for Spanish-speaking youngsters and others whose primary language is not English. Readers are encouraged to write to the Texas Board of Education for the complete text; in addition, a PDF file can be located at www.tea.state.tx.us/teks.

Kindergarten Standards

Kindergarten students engage in many activities that help develop their oral language skills and help them to begin to read and write.

Reading/Print Awareness

The student is expected to:

1. recognize that print represents spoken language and conveys meaning such as his/her own name and signs such as Exit and Danger (K–1);

2. know that print moves left to right across the page and top to bottom (K–1);

3. understand that written words are separated by spaces (K–1);

4. know the difference between individual letters and printed words (K–1);

5. know the difference between capital and lowercase letters (K–1);

6. recognize how readers use capitalization and punctuation to comprehend (K–1);

7. understand that spoken words are represented in written language by specific sequences of letters (K–1);

8. recognize that different parts of a book such as cover, title page, and table of contents offer information (K–1).

Reading/Phonological Awareness

The student is expected to:

1. demonstrate the concept of a word by dividing spoken sentences into individual words (K–1);

2. identify, segment, and combine syllables within spoken words such as by clapping syllables and moving manipulatives to represent syllables in words (K–1);

3. produce rhyming words and distinguish rhyming words from non-rhyming words (K–1);

4. identify and isolate the initial and final sounds of a spoken word (K–1);

5. blend sounds to make spoken words such as moving manipulatives to blend phonemes in a spoken word (K–1);

6. segment one-syllable spoken words into individual phonemes, clearly producing beginning, medial, and final sounds (K–1).

Reading/Letter-Sound Relationships

The student is expected to:

1. name and identify each letter of the alphabet (K–1);

2. understand that written words are composed of letters that represent sounds (K–1);

3. learn and apply letter-sound correspondences of a set of consonants and vowels to begin to read (K–1).

First Grade Standards

In Grade 1, students continue to develop their oral language and communication skills and move to becoming independent readers and writers.

Students learn most of the common letter-sound correspondences and use this knowledge to decode written words.

Reading/Print Awareness

The student is expected to:

1. recognize that print represents spoken language and conveys meaning such as his/her own name and signs such as Exit and Danger (K–1);

2. know that print moves left to right across the page and top to bottom (K–1);

3. understand that written words are separated by spaces (K–1);

4. know the difference between individual letters and printed words (K–1);

5. know the order of the alphabet (K–1);

6. know the difference between capital and lowercase letters (K–1);

7. recognize how readers use capitalization and punctuation to comprehend (K–1);

8. understand that spoken words are represented in written language by specific sequences of letters (K–1);

9. recognize that different parts of a book such as cover, title page, and table of contents offer information (K–1);

10. recognize that there are correct spellings for words (1);

11. recognize the distinguishing features of a paragraph (1).

Reading/Phonological Awareness

The student is expected to:

1. demonstrate the concept of what a word is by dividing spoken sentences into individual words (K–1);

2. identify, segment and combine syllables within spoken words such as by clapping syllables and moving manipulatives to represent syllables in words (K–1);

3. produce rhyming words and distinguish rhyming words from non-rhyming words (K–1);

4. identify and isolate the initial and final sound of a spoken word (K–1);

5. blend sounds to make spoken words, including three and four phoneme words, through ways such as moving manipulatives to blend phonemes in a spoken word (1);

6. segment one-syllable spoken words into individual phonemes, including three and four phoneme words, clearly producing beginning, medial, and final sounds (K–1).

Reading/Letter-Sound Relationships

The student is expected to:

1. name and identify each letter of the alphabet (K–1);

2. understand that written words are composed of letters that represent sounds (K–1);

3. learn and apply letter-sound correspondences of a set of consonants and vowels to begin to read (K–1);

4. learn and apply the most common letter-sound correspondences, including the sounds represented by single letters (consonants and vowels); consonant blends such as *bl, st, tr*; consonant digraphs such as *th, sh, ck*; and vowel digraphs and diphthongs such as *ea, ie, ee* (1);

5. blend initial letter-sounds with common vowel spelling patterns to read words (1–3);

6. decode by using letter-sound correspondences within regularly spelled words (1–3);

7. use letter-sound knowledge to read decodable texts (engaging and coherent texts in which most of the words are comprised of an accumulating sequence of letter-sound correspondences being taught) (1).

Reading/Word Identification

The student is expected to:

1. decode by using all letter-sound correspondences within a word (1–3);

2. use common spelling patterns to read words (1);

3. use structural cues to recognize words such as compounds, base words, and inflections such *as -s, -es, -ed, -ing* (1–2);

4. identify multisyllabic words by using common syllable patterns (1–3);

5. recognize high frequency irregular words such as *said, was, where,* and *is* (1–2);

6. use knowledge of word order (syntax) and context to support word identification and confirm word meaning (1–3);

7. read both regular and irregular words automatically such as through multiple opportunities to read and reread (1–3).

Writing/Spelling

The student is expected to:

1. write his/her name and other important words (K–1);

2. write each letter of the alphabet, both capital and lowercase, using correct formation, appropriate size, and spacing (1);

3. use phonological knowledge to map sounds to letters and write messages (K–1);

4. write with more proficient spelling of regularly spelled patterns such as consonant-vowel-consonant (CVC)—*cat, hot, but,* consonant-vowel-consonant-silent e (CVCe)—*hope, game, mice,* and one-syllable words with blends—*drop, slip, when* (1–3);

5. write with more proficient spelling of inflectional endings such as plurals and verb tenses (1–2);

6. spell single syllable words that have *r*-controlled vowels such as *burn* or *star*; that have final consonants *l, f,* and *s* such as in *miss* or *doll*; and that have *ck* as the final consonant such as *buck* (1);

7. use resources to find correct spelling, synonyms, and replacement words (1–3);

8. use conventional spelling of familiar words in final draft (1).

Second Grade Standards

In Grade 2, students read and write independently. Second grade students recognize a large number of words automatically, and use a variety of word identification strategies to figure out words they do not immediately recognize.

Reading/Word Identification

The student is expected to:

1. decode by using all letter-sound correspondences within a word (1–3);

2. blend initial letter-sound with common vowel spelling patterns to read words (1–3);

3. recognize high frequency irregular words such as: *said, was, where,* and *is* (1–2);

4. identify multisyllabic words by using common syllable patterns (1–3);

5. use structural cues to recognize words such as compounds, base words, and inflections such as *-s, -es, -ed,* and *-ing* (1–2);

6. use structural cues such as prefixes and suffixes to recognize words, for example, *un-* and *-ly* (2);

7. use knowledge of word order (syntax); and content to support word identification and confirm word meaning (1–3);

8. read both regular and irregular words automatically such as through multiple opportunities to read and reread (1–3);

Writing/Spelling

The student is expected to:

1. use resources to find correct spelling, synonyms, and replacement words (1–3);

2. write with more proficient spelling of regularly spelled patterns such as consonant-vowel-consonant (CVC)—*cat, hot, but,* consonant-vowel-consonant-silent e (CVCe)—*hope, gone, mice,* and one syllable words with blends—*drop, slip, when* (1–3);

3. write with more proficient spelling of inflectional endings, including plurals and verb tenses (1–2);

4. write with more proficient use of orthographic patterns and rules such as: *keep/cap, sack/book, out/cow,* consonant doubling, dropping *e* and changing *y* to *i* (2).

Third Grade Standards

In Grade 3, students read and write more independently than in any previous grade and spend significant blocks of time engaged in reading and writing on their own as well as assigned tasks and projects.

Reading/Word Identification

The student is expected to:

1. decode by using all letter-sound correspondences within a word (1–3);

2. blend initial letter-sounds with common vowel spelling patterns to read words (1–3);

3. identify multisyllabic words by using common syllable patterns (1–3);

4. use root words and other structural cues such as prefixes and suffixes and derivational endings to recognize words (3);

5. use knowledge of word order (syntax) and context to support word identification and confirm word meaning (1–3);

6. read both regular and irregular words automatically such as through multiple opportunities to read and reread (1–3).

Writing/Spelling

The student is expected to:

1. write with more proficient spelling of regularly spelled patterns such as consonant-vowel-consonant (CVC)—*cat, hot, but,* consonant-vowel-consonant-silent e—*hope, game, mice,* and one syllable words with blends—*drop, slip, when* (1–3);

2. spell multisyllabic words using regularly spelled phonogram patterns (3);

3. write with more proficient spelling of inflectional endings, including plurals and past tense and words that drop the final *e* when such endings as *-ed, -ing,* or *-able* are added (3);

4. write with more proficient use of orthographic patterns and rules such as *oil/toy, match/speech, badge/cage,* consonant doubling, dropping *e* and changing *y* to *i* (3);

5. write with more proficient spelling of contractions, compounds and homonyms such as *hair/hare, bear/bare* (3);

6. write with accurate spelling of syllable constructions such as closed, open, consonants before *-le* and syllable boundary patterns (3–6);

7. spell words ending in *-tion* and *-sion* such as *station* and *procession* (3);

8. use resources to find correct spelling, synonyms or replacement words (1–3).

Fourth Grade Standards

In Grade 4, students spend significant blocks of time engaged in reading and writing independently. Fourth grade students read with a growing interest in a wide variety of topics and adjust their reading approach to various forms of texts.

Reading/Word Identification

The student is expected to:

1. apply knowledge of letter-sound correspondences, language structure, and context to recognize words (4–8);

2. use structural analysis to identify root words with prefixes such as *dis-, non-, in-,* and suffixes such as *-ness, -tion,* and *-able* (4–6);

3. locate the meanings, pronunciations, and derivations of unfamiliar words using dictionaries, glossaries, and other sources (4–8).

Writing/Spelling

The student is expected to:

1. write with accurate spelling of syllable constructions including closed, open, consonant before *-le* and syllable boundary patterns (3–6);

2. write with accurate spelling of roots such as *drink, speak, read,* or *happy,* inflections such as those that change tense or number suffixes such as *-able* or *-less* and prefixes such as *re-* and *un-* (4–6);

3. use regular and irregular plurals correctly (4–6);

4. use adjectives (comparative and superlative forms); and adverbs appropriately to make writing vivid and precise (4–6).

Fifth Grade Standards

In Grade 5, students refine and master previous learned knowledge skills in increasingly complex presentations, reading selections, and written composition. Children read from classic and contemporary selections and informational texts.

Reading/Word Identification

The student is expected to:

1. apply knowledge of letter sound correspondences, language structure, and context to recognize words (4–8);

2. use structural analysis to identify root words with prefixes such as *dis-, non-,* and *in-;* and suffixes such as *-ness, -tion,* and *-able* (4–6);

3. locate the meanings, pronunciations and derivation of unfamiliar words using dictionaries, glossaries, and other sources (4–6);

4. determine meanings of derivatives by applying knowledge of the meaning of root words such as *like, pay,* or *happy,* and affixes such as *dis-, pre-,* and *un-* (4–8);

5. use adjectives (comparative and superlative forms) and adverbs appropriately to make writing vivid or precise (4–6).

THE CONTINUUM APPROACH[1]

The Continuum (continuous phases) of Children's Development in Early Reading and Writing was developed as a result of the thinking of teacher

---

1. SOURCE: *Learning to Read and Write: Developmentally Appropriate Practices for Young Children.* (1998). A joint position statement of the International Reading Association and National Association for the Education of Young Children. Copyright 1998 by IRA and NAEYC. All rights reserved. Reprinted with permission.

trainers, researchers, policy makers, classroom teachers, parents, and consultants from the U.S. Department of Education. One of the important aspects of the Continuum is that it points out clearly that learning to read and write involves the participation of parents and family members as well as that of child and teacher. Following are the key points for each of the five phases as outlined in a joint position statement of the International Reading Association and the National Association for the Education of Young Children (adopted 1998).

Continuum of Children's Development in Early Reading and Writing

Phase 1: Awareness and Exploration (Goals for Preschool)

Children explore their environment and build the foundations for learning to read and write.

Children can

- Enjoy listening to and discussing storybooks
- Understand that print carries a message
- Engage in reading and writing attempts
- Identify labels and signs in their environment
- Participate in rhyming games
- Identify some letters and make some letter-sound matches
- Use known letters or approximations of letters to represent written language (especially meaningful words like their name and phrases such as "I love you")

What teachers do

- Share books with children, including Big Books, and model reading behaviors
- Talk about letters by name and sound
- Establish a literacy-rich environment
- Reread favorite stories
- Engage children in language games
- Promote literacy-related play activities
- Encourage children to experiment with writing

What parents and family can do

- Talk with children, engage them in conversation, give names of things, show interest in what child says
- Read and reread stories with predictable text to children
- Encourage children to recount experiences and describe ideas and events that are important to them
- Visit the library regularly
- Provide opportunities for the child to draw and print, using markers, crayons, and pencils

*Phase 2: Experimental Reading and
Writing (Goals for Kindergarten)*

Children develop basic concepts of print and begin to engage in and experiment with reading and writing.

Kindergartners can

- Enjoy being read to and themselves retell simple narrative stories or informational texts
- Use descriptive language to explain and explore
- Recognize letters and letter-sound matches
- Show familiarity with rhyming and beginning sounds
- Understand left-to-right and top-to-bottom orientation and familiar concepts in print
- Match spoken words with written ones
- Begin to write letters of the alphabet and some high frequency words
- What teachers do
- Encourage children to talk about reading and writing experiences
- Provide many opportunities for children to explore and identify sound-symbol relationships in meaningful context
- Help children to segment spoken words into individual sounds and blend sounds into whole words (for example, by slowly writing a word and saying its sound)
- Frequently read interesting and conceptually rich stories to children
- Provide daily opportunities for children to write
- Help children to build a sight vocabulary
- Create a literacy-rich environment for children to engage independently in reading and writing

What parents and family members can do

- Daily read and reread narrative and informational stories to children
- Encourage children's attempts at reading and writing
- Allow children to participate in activities that involve writing and reading (for example, cooking, making grocery lists)
- Play games that involve specific directions (such as "Simon Says")
- Have conversation with children during mealtimes and throughout the day

Phase 3: Early Reading and Writing (Goals for First Grade)

Children begin to read simple stories and can write on a topic that is meaningful to them.

First graders can

- Read and retell familiar stories
- Use strategies (rereading, predicting, questioning, contextualizing) when comprehension breaks down
- Orally read with reasonable fluency

- Use letter-sound associations, word parts, and context to identify new words
- Identify an increasing number of words by sight
- Sound out and represent all substantial sounds in spelling a word
- Write about topics that are personally meaningful
- Attempt to use some punctuation and capitalization

What teachers do

- Support the development of vocabulary by reading daily to the children, transcribing their language, and selecting materials that expand children's knowledge and language development
- Model strategies and provide practice for identifying unknown words
- Give children opportunities for independent reading and writing practice
- Read, write, and discuss a range of different text types (poems, informational books)
- Introduce new words and teach strategies for learning to spell new words
- Demonstrate and model strategies to use when comprehension breaks down
- Help children build lists of commonly used words from their writing

What parents and family members can do

- Talk about favorite storybooks
- Read to children and encourage them to read to you
- Suggest that children write to friends and relatives
- Bring to a parent-teacher conference evidence of what your child can do in writing and reading
- Encourage children to share what they have learned about writing and reading

Phase 4: Transitional Reading and Writing (Goals for Second Grade)

Children begin to read more fluently and write various text forms using simple and more complex sentences.

Second graders can

- Read with greater fluency
- Use strategies more efficiently (rereading, questioning, and so on) when comprehension breaks down
- Use word identification strategies with greater facility to unlock unknown words
- Identify an increasing number of words by sight
- Write about a range of topics to suit different audiences
- Use common letter patterns and critical features to spell words
- Punctuate simple sentences correctly and proofread their own work
- Spend time reading daily and use reading to research topic

What teachers do

- Create a climate that fosters analytic, evaluative, and reflective thinking
- Teach children to write in multiple forms (stories, information, poems)
- Ensure that children read a range of texts for a variety of purposes
- Teach revising, editing, and proofreading skills
- Teach strategies for spelling new and difficult words
- Model enjoyment of reading

What parents and family members can do

- Continue to read to children and encourage them to read to you
- Engage children in activities that require reading and writing
- Become involved in school activities
- Show children your interest in their learning by displaying their written work
- Visit a library regularly
- Support your child's specific hobby or interest with reading material and references

Phase 5: Independent and Productive Reading and Writing (Goals for Third Grade)

Children continue to extend and refine their reading and writing to suit varying purposes and audiences.

Third graders can

- Read fluently and enjoy reading
- Use a range of strategies when drawing meaning from the text
- Use word identification strategies appropriately and automatically when encountering unknown words
- Recognize and discuss elements of different text structures
- Make critical connections between texts
- Write expressively in many different forms (stories, poems, reports)
- Use a rich variety of vocabulary and sentences appropriate to text forms
- Revise and edit their own writing during and after composing
- Spell words correctly in final spelling drafts

What teachers do

- Provide opportunities daily for children to read, examine, and critically evaluate narrative and expository texts
- Continue to create a climate that fosters critical reading and personal response
- Teach children to examine ideas in context
- Encourage children to use writing as a tool for thinking and learning
- Extend children's knowledge of the correct use of writing conventions
- Emphasize the importance of correct spelling in finished written projects
- Create a climate that engages all children as a community of literate learners

What parents and family members can do

- Continue to support children's learning and interests by visiting the library and bookstores with them
- Find ways to highlight children's progress in reading and writing
- Stay in regular contact with your child's teachers about activities and progress in reading and writing
- Encourage children to use and enjoy print for many purposes (such as recipes, directions, games, and sports)
- Build a love of language in all its forms and engage children in conversation

Resource B: A Synopsis of Phonics Instructional Skills

Consonants: One of two categories of sounds in English that are made by touching part of the mouth or lip to each other in speech.

Single consonants generally represent a single sound.

Voiceless	Voiced
p- pig, dip	b- bad, rib
t- tent, met	d- dad, lid
k- kite, make	g- get, rug
f- fun, loaf	g = j, giant
s- smell, maps	s = z, has
h- hen	v- very, live
j- jump	
z- zoom	
(zh) azure	

Consonant Irregularities: Consonants may have more than one sound.

When "g" is followed by "a," "o," or "u," it has the hard sound of g. When it is followed by an "e," "i," or "y," it has the soft sound associated with j.

g = g	game	gone	gum
g = j	gentle	ginger	gym

The letter "s" may have four different pronunciations.

s = s, say	s = z, his	s = sh, sure	s = zh, treasure

The letter combination *ph* is pronounced as *f* (*phone*, al*ph*abet, hy*ph*en, etc.).

In English, the letter *q* is always followed by u (*quick, question, queen*, etc.).

"Que" at the end of a word has the sound of /k/; usually the "que" is blended with the preceding syllable (*antique, technique, opaque*, etc.).

"D" has the sound of /d/ in most words (*did, doll, don't, do, dog*, etc.). Rarely does it have the sound of /j/ as in *individual, graduate, cordial*.

Silent Consonants:

Many English words contain both silent consonants and silent vowels. The following rules or generalizations are fairly consistent and therefore easily learned.

In words containing double consonants (*letter, message, happen*) only one consonant is sounded.

In words beginning with *kn* (*knew, knee, knife*) the k is usually silent.

The combination *gh* is usually silent when preceded by the vowel *i* (*light, night, sigh*, etc.).

In words beginning with *wr* (*write, wreck, wren*) the *w* is usually silent.

In words ending in *ten* (*often, listen, tighten*) the *t* is usually silent.

In words containing *ck* (*sack, black, pick*) the *c* is usually silent.

In words ending in *mb* (*thumb, lamb, climb*) the *b* is usually silent.

Initial Consonant Blend Sounds

bl- black	gl- glass	sl-slow	str- strap
br- brown	gr- green	sm- smell	sw- sweet
cl- climb	pl- place	sn- snow	th- thin
cr- cross	pr- pray	sp- spill	thr- through
dr- drop	sc- scar	spl- splash	tr- trace
dw- dwell	scr- scream	spr- spring	tw- twins
fl- fly	shr- shrug	squ- square	
fr- free	sk- skill	st- start	

Consonant Digraphs are a combination of two letters that results in one speech sound. A digraph may have more than one pronunciation resulting in a single sound in each case (*ch* = *k* for *chorus*; *sh* for *chef*; *ch* for *church*).

sh- shall	wh- when	ch- church	voiced th- those	qu-/kw
			unvoiced th- the	quit

Ending Digraphs

nd- sand	nk- thank	nt- want	rk- dark	rt- dart

Vowels are "opened mouthed" letters of the alphabet that are not consonants. Every word or syllable must contain at least one vowel.

Vowels are generally described as being long or short. Long vowels have more stress and are pronounced as the five vowel letters of the alphabet are pronounced ("they say their name"). Short vowels have less stress and do not say the letter names.

Vowel Generalizations

Although there are only five letters that are always vowels (*a, e, i, o, u*) and two letters (*y* and *w*) that are sometimes vowels, there are at least nineteen different vowel sounds.

/a/—cat	/a/—make	/ar/—care	/a/—father	/e/—bet	/e/—tree
/i/—in	/i/—eye	/ir/—fear	/o/—not	/o/—no	/o/—fall
/oi/—noise	/ou/—mouse	/oo/—cook	/oo/—toot	/u/—cut	/yoo/—use
/ur/—fern					

A single vowel in a medial position (c/v/c) usually has a short *e* sound.

man	set	bid	but	lot

Exceptions

When the vowel *o* is followed by *ld* it usually has a long vowel sound: *sold, old, bold, told,* etc.

When the vowel *i* is followed by *nd, gh,* or *ld* it often has the long vowel sound: *kind, fight, mild,* etc.

The vowel a will take on the sound of aw when followed by *l, ll, w, u*: *talk, ball, draw, because,* etc.

When a single vowel is followed by an *r* it is pronounced as a glide ("controlled *r*"): *car, tart, her, for,* etc.

The spelling ir is usually pronounced *ur* (*bird = burd*) except when followed by a final *e* (*fire, tire, hire,* etc.)

When two vowels come together in a word, the first vowel is generally long, and the second vowel is silent ("the first one does the talking and the second the walking").

team	people	goal	mail	feed	suit	receive

When an *e* appears at the end of a word, it usually makes the vowel before it long.

game	eve	write	hope	use	village

When the only vowel in a word comes at the end, it is usually long: *he, hi(gh), no, free, blow,* etc.

When a one-syllable word ends with *y*, it generally takes on the long sound of *i*. When y ends a word of two or more syllables, then it takes on the sound of long *e*.

y = /i/	try	why	fly	shy	my
y = /e/	baby	funny	windy	restlessly	January

Unaccented vowels are similar in sound, and are indicated in many dictionaries by a schwa (upside down e, or /ǝ/): capit*a*l, oft*e*n, multipl*y*, hum*o*r, etc.

Diphthongs are two vowels together that produce a new single sound unlike the short or long vowel sounds.

The diphthongs *oi* and *oy* have the same sound. Generally when this sound is heard at the end of the word it is spelled *oy* (*boy, toy, employ,* etc). When it is at the beginning or in the medial position, it is spelled *oi* (*coin, oil, toil,* etc.).

The diphthongs ou and ow have the same sound. Generally when that sound appears at the end of a word it is spelled *ow* (*how, chow, plow,* etc.); at other times it is spelled *ou* (*house, cloud, out,* etc.).

Syllabication: **Dividing Words Into Syllables**

Rule 1: There are as many syllables in a word as there are vowel sounds. It is the vowel sound that determines the number of syllables, not the number of vowels seen in the word.

go—1 vowel seen	cheese—3 vowels seen	precaution—5 vowels seen
1 vowel heard	1 vowel heard	3 vowels heard

Rule 2: **(vc/cv)** Divide words between double vowels, or between two consonants other than blends or digraphs.

lit-tle	sud-den	com-mand	tun-nel	vol-ley
can-dy	bas-ket	un-der	des-pite	res-cue

Rule 3: **(v/cv)** When a single consonant comes between two vowels, the consonant generally goes with the second vowel.

be-gin	a-lone	be-fore	cel-e-brate	ba-by
fro-zen	ho-tel	di-rect	a-bout	hu-man

Rule 4: As a general rule do not divide consonant digraphs and consonant blends.

teach-er	weath-er	a-gree	ath-lete	coun-try
ma-chine	moth-er	A-pril	de-stroy	De-troit

Rule 5: Word endings *-ble, -cle, -dle, -gle, -kle, -ple, -le, -zle,* constitute the final syllable.

ta-ble	mus-cle	can-dle	sin-gle	pic-kle
ti-tle	no-ble	pur-ple	tur-tle	puz-zle

Rule 6: Prefixes and suffixes generally form separate syllables.

re-do	un-fair	hap-pi-ness	pre-heat-ed	help-less
ex-cite-ment	for-give-ness	trans-port-able	like-ly	see-ing

Structural Analysis

Prefixes are one or more syllables added to the beginning of a word to give it a new or different meaning.

read–reread	do–undo	like–dislike	cast–forecast	pod–tripod

Suffixes are one or more syllables placed at the ending of a word that changes the grammatical meaning of the word. In some cases, the suffix makes a radical change in the meaning of the word (*hope–hopeless*).

happy–happily	luck–lucky	good–goodness	go–going	talk–talked

One-vowel words ending in a single consonant usually double that consonant before adding an ending that starts with a vowel.

run–running	stop–stopped	beg–beggar	big–biggest	drug–druggist

Plurals are words that mean more than one person, place, or thing. Plurals are formed in one of three ways depending on the ending of the root word.

1. Most plurals are formed by adding an *s* at the end of the word.

car–cars	boy–boys	girl–girls	bird–birds	pet–pets

2. When a noun ends in *-s, -ss, -ch, -sh,* or *-x,* the plural is formed by adding *-es.*

bus–buses	glass–glasses	lunch–lunches	dish–dishes	box–boxes

3. When a noun ends in *-y,* change the *-y* to *i* and add *-es.*

fly–flies	army–armies	body–bodies	lady–ladies	baby–babies

Contractions are single words formed by combining two words and omitting a letter or letters, and adding an apostrophe.

I will–I'll	is not–isn't	will not–won't	you are–you're	I am–I'm

Compound Words are formed by combining two smaller words into one. The meaning is derived from the combination of the two words.

doghouse	downtown	uphill	wetlands	northwest

Synonyms are words that have the same, or nearly the same, meaning as other words.

bright–sunny	sad–somber	run–trot	house–home	baby–infant

Homonyms are words that have the same pronunciation but different spellings and meanings.

meet–meat	week–weak	road–rode	ate–eight	our–hour

Homographs are words with identical spelling but with different meanings, sometimes with different pronunciations.

lead–lead	live–live	read–read	wind–wind	object–object

Resource C: Reading Skills Checklist

Reading Skills Checklist

Child's name _____

PREREADING SKILLS:

(When child knows and can apply the following skills, check box at left)

	Knows parts of book (back, front, illustration, print)
	Understands that print goes from left to right across the page
	Understands that print goes from top to bottom on the page
	Distinguishes printed words and letters
	Understands that printed words stand for spoken words
	Identifies and recognizes characters in the book
	Points to words in the book
	Retells story in proper order
	Recites some of the letters in the alphabet
	Recognizes his or her name in print
	Uses pictures, context, or repeated words to predict upcoming words
	Enjoys looking through books on own and without supervision
	Enjoys some books more than others
	Is able to produce simple rhyming words (*boy–joy, tell–bell, other–mother*)

ALPHABET SKILLS:

(When child knows and can apply the following skills, check box at left)

	Recites the letters of the alphabet in order
	Recognizes individual letters by sight
	Knows differences between capital and small letters
	Matches small letters with capital letters

	Knows the alphabet is composed of consonants and vowels
	Locates individual letters within words
	Knows written letters represent spoken sound
	Writes all the letters of the alphabet in order
	Writes all the letters in manuscript
	Writes all the letters in cursive handwriting
	Able to alphabetize by the first letter
	Able to alphabetize to the second letter
	Able to alphabetize to the third letter

CONSONANT SKILLS:

(When child knows and can apply the following skills, check box at left)

	Identify, by name, all the letters of the alphabet
	Distinguished vowels from consonant sounds and letters
	Knows sounds of individual consonants
	Knows sounds of individual consonants in the initial position (*b* as in *book*, *c* as in *cat*, *m* as in *mother*, *z* as in *zoo*, etc.)
	Knows sounds of individual consonants in final position (*k* as in *black*, *s* as in *us*, *n* as in *gun*, *t* as in *silent*, etc.)
	Knows sounds of initial consonant blends (*shop, blue, tree, when, chest, clam, glue, drip, small, draw, stop, play, free, then, flag, spell, snow, swell, grass*)
	Knows sounds of consonant blends in final position (*peach, push, north, fast, ask, grasp*)
	Knows the sounds of triple blends (*street, school, through, spree, splash, Chris*)
	Knows sounds of initial consonant digraphs (*shall, this, chair, chorus*)
	Knows sounds of final consonant digraphs (*bang, junk, hung, (qu as kw) queen*)
	Knows that *c* has the sound of *k* when followed by *a, o, u* (*cat, come, cube*)
	Knows that *c* has the sound of *s* when followed by *i, e, y* (*city, cent, cypress*)

	Knows that *ph* has the sound of *f* (*orphans, phones, graph*)
	Knows that *que* at end of word has sound of *k* (*antique, critique, technique*)
	Knows that in words containing a double consonant, only one sound is heard (*ladder, message, dinner, yellow, kitten*)
	Knows that when words begin with *kn*, the *k* is usually silent (*knew, knee, knock*)
	Knows that the *gh* is usually silent when followed by a vowel (*night, ought, sigh*)
	Knows that in words beginning with *wr* the *w* is usually silent (*wren, write, wrong*)
	Knows that in words ending in the syllable *ten* the *t* is silent (*often, listen, fasten*)
	Knows that in words containing *ck* the *c* is generally silent (*neck, block, pick*)
	Knows that in words ending in *mb* the *b* is usually silent (*bomb, limb, lamb*)
	Knows that *s* can be pronounced in three ways (*s = s—sells, s = z—his, s = zh—sugar*)

VOWEL SKILLS

(When child knows and can apply the following skills, check box at left)

	Knows the letter names of the vowels
	Knows that words are composed of vowel and consonant sounds
	Knows that every word must have at least one vowel sound
	Knows that each syllable in a word contains one vowel sound (*go, mo-ther, clear-ly, un-der-stand-ing, com-mu-ni-ca-tion*)
	Knows that a single vowel, unless at the end, is generally short (*cat, stop, first, duck, chest*)
	Knows that when a vowel appears at the end of a word it is generally long (*no, so, by, why, me, she*)
	Blends vowel and consonant sounds orally to make words
	Distinguishes (hears) short vowel sounds from long vowel sounds (*mad—made, pen–eat, tin–time, on–open, bus–blue, yes–by*)

	Distinguishes (hears) beginning, middle, and ending sounds in words
	Counts (claps) the number of sounds or syllables in a word
	Identifies and reproduces rhyming words from other words
	Knows that some words may sound the same but have different spellings and meanings (*there–their, hear–here, two–to–too, ate–eight, see–sea*)
	Knows that one vowel sound (long or short) may be spelled in different ways (*a = may, make, eight, they, forte,* etc.; *e = end, many, said, head, bury,* etc.)
	Knows that when two vowels come together, the first usually has a long sound and the second is generally silent (*boat, chain, beat, feed, grain*)
	Knows that when an *e* appears at the end of a word it usually makes the vowel before it long (*hat–hate, hid–hide, past–paste, pin–pine, mad–made*)
	Knows that when *-ay* appears at the end of a word it usually has the sound of long *a* (*may, pray, today, clay, spray*)
	Knows that when *y* appears at the end of a one-syllable word it generally has the sound of long *i* (*by, cry, sky, try, spry*)
	Knows that when *y* appears at the end of a word with two or more syllables it generally has the sound of long *e* (*funny, merry, honestly, lucky, January*)
	Knows that when the vowel *o* is followed by *-ld* it usually has the long sound (*old, bold, cold, fold, sold*)
	Knows that when the vowel *i* is followed by *-nd, -gh,* and *-ld* it usually has the long sound (*find, light, wild, right, behind*)
	Knows that a vowel followed by an *r* results in a blended sound, which is neither a short or long vowel (*farm, person, north, first, thrift*)
	Knows that *a = /aw/* sound when followed by *l, ll, w,* and *u* (*talk, wall, draw, haul*)
	Knows that a diphthong is two adjacent vowels, each of which contributes to the sound heard (*house, owl, boy, oil*)
	Knows that the diphthongs *oi* and *oy* have the same sound and the diphthongs *ow* and *ou* have the same sounds (*boil–boy, noise–joy; round–clown, cloud–now*)
	Can distinguish (pronounce correctly) most words with long and short *oo* words (long sound = *boot, loose, tooth,* etc.; short sound = *book, good, took,* etc.)

SYLLABICATION & STRUCTURAL ANALYSIS SKILLS

(When child knows and can apply the following skills, check box at left)

	Knows that there are as many syllables in a word as there are vowel sounds
	Knows that many words contain silent letters (*know, bomb, little, right, are*)
	Knows that when prefixes and suffixes are added to a word it changes the meaning of the word (*happy–unhappy, go–going, obey–disobey, tooth–toothless*)
	Knows common word endings sounds of *ed* (*ed* as in *wanted*; *ed* = *d* as in *laughed*; *ed* = *t* as in *liked*)
	Knows the common word endings *-er, -est, -ing, -en, -able* (*better, highest, going, soften, capable*)
	Knows that when a one-vowel word ends with a single consonant the final consonant is generally doubled when adding an ending (*run–running, stop–stopped, beg–begged, dim–dimmed, can–canned*)
	Knows that compound words are made of smaller words and can divide them between the two words (*up-on, after-noon, base-ball, row-boat, air-port*)
	Knows that when there is a single consonant between two vowels (v/c/v), the vowel generally goes with the first syllable (*ti-ger, po-lice, wa-ter, spi-der, pu-pil*)
	Knows that when there is a double consonant or two consonants together, the syllable break comes between the two consonants (*lit-tle, har-bor, cin-der*)
	Knows that when a prefix or suffix is attached to a word, it is generally treated as a separate syllable (*re-load-ing, pre-heat-ed, hope-less-ness, ex-cite-ment*)
	Knows that when dividing words into syllables that the consonant blends and digraphs generally stay together (*teach-er, coun-try, a-gree, wea-ther, mo-ther*)
	Knows that *-ble, -cle, -dle, -gle, -kle, -ple, -tle, -zle* constitute the final syllable in a word (*mar-ble, mus-cle, han-dle, sin-gle, an-kle, tem-ple, ket-tle, puz-zle*)
	Knows that most plurals are formed by adding an s to the root word (*cars, boys*)
	Knows that when a word ends in *-s, -ss, -ch, -sh, -x*, the plural is formed by adding *es* (*bus-buses, dress-dresses, lunch-lunches, fish-fishes, box-boxes*)
	Knows the contractions: *I'm, I've, isn't can't, don't, isn't, let's, we've*

Resource D: Checkpoints for Parents of Preschoolers

CHECKPOINTS FOR PARENTS OF PRESCHOOLERS

Preparing for Reading

- ✓ Do I read to my child every day?
- ✓ Do I praise my child for good speech patterns and conduct?
- ✓ Do I have picture books and rhyming books around the house?
- ✓ Do I enjoy reading myself and set an example for my child?
- ✓ Do I talk to my child about things that I have read?
- ✓ Am I a good listener and ask the children questions about what they think about stories?
- ✓ Do I keep television watching to a minimum or restrict it to certain programs and hours?
- ✓ Do I visit the library or take my child to story hour on a regular basis?
- ✓ Do I allow my child to pick out his/her own book at the library?
- ✓ Do I allow my child to point to objects in the book?
- ✓ Do I encourage my child to turn the pages of the book?
- ✓ Does the child have any books he/she can call his/her own?
- ✓ Do I talk about objects in books?
- ✓ Do I ask my child questions about things I have read to him/her?
- ✓ Do I tell stories to my child on a regular basis?
- ✓ Do I sing or recite rhymes and/or songs with my child?
- ✓ Do I read to my child things I see every day (signs in store windows, traffic signs, cereal boxes, etc.)?
- ✓ Does the child have a work area with pencils, paper, crayons, where he/she can work?

Social and Emotional Preparation Learning

- ✓ Does my child like to explore and try new things?
- ✓ Is my child learning to do things by him- or herself and work by him- or herself?
- ✓ Does my child know his/her name and address?
- ✓ Does my child eat a balanced diet?
- ✓ Does my child receive regular medical and dental care?
- ✓ Does my child get plenty of rest and sleep well?
- ✓ Does my child like to play outside and with other children?
- ✓ Do I join in my child's activities and allow him/her to join in mine?
- ✓ Do I recognize my child's successes and praise the child for success?

Glossaries

PHONOLOGICAL TERMS GLOSSARY

Accent. The part of the word that receives greater emphasis or stress in pronunciation. Dictionaries generally place a mark over the accented syllable in a word to assist pronunciation: *gó-ing, for-gét, un-der-stánd-ing.*

Affix. A syllable or syllables—a prefix or suffix—added to the beginning or ending of a word to change its meaning: *undo, renew, going, lovely.*

Alliteration. The repetition of the same sound, usually of a consonant, at the beginning of two or more words: the *sun smiles, the green grass grows.*

Allomorph. One or two forms of the same morpheme. The /z/ as represented by *s* as in *boys*, the /s/ represented by *s* as in *cats*, and the /z/ as represented by *es* are all forms, or allomorphs, of the "plural" morpheme.

Alphabetic awareness. Knowledge of the letters of the alphabet and knowledge that letters of the alphabet represent sounds of the spoken language.

Antonym. A word that has the opposite meaning of another word: *tall–short, happy–sad, up–down.*

Compound word. A word made up of two separate words: *cowboy, street-car, underground.*

Consonant blends. Two or more consonants that come together to produce a new phoneme that results from a blend of the consonant sounds: *black, trace, screw.*

Consonant phoneme. One of two groups of sounds found in English (the other being vowel phonemes). Consonants are produced when outgoing breath is stopped or halted and then released. There are approximately twenty-four consonant phonemes, plus blends and digraphs.

Context. The environment, or circumstances, of a spoken or written word that often affects its meaning and helps one guess the word's meaning.

Contraction. Two words made into one for ease of pronunciation. An apostrophe is used in place of the missing letter or letters: *I'll, don't, shouldn't.*

Decoding. The process of changing written or printed language into spoken sounds. Decoding is a synonym for reading.

Diacritical mark. A dictionary marking placed above, under, or next to a syllable in a word to indicate pronunciation or stress: home, át, read, âre.

Dialect. A regional version of a language that differs in pronunciation, grammar, or vocabulary from standard speech patterns or standard usage.

Digraph. A combination of letters used to spell a single sound. Digraphs can be vowel digraphs (*piece, coat, read*) or consonant digraphs (*the, physics, sick*).

Diphthong. A sequence of two vowels or semivowels within the same syllable pronounced as a single (joined) vowel: *boil, boys, how.*

Encoding. The process of changing spoken language into printed or written language. Encoding is a synonym for spelling.

Etymology. The origin of a word. The study of the history of a word from its earliest recorded forms to its present spelling and usage.

Fluency. The ease with which one can read or translate printed material into speech.

Grapheme. A written letter of the alphabet. The sum of the letters and letter combinations that can represent phonemes or sounds of the language.

Homograph. A word spelled, or written, the same as another word, but with a different pronunciation and meaning: *lead–lead, bow–bow, read–read.*

Homophone. A word that is pronounced the same as another word but is spelled differently and has a different meaning: *their–there, here–hear, to–too–two.* Another name for a homophone is *homonym.*

Invented spelling. A spelling method that writers (generally children) use to approximate the proper spelling of a word that they may not know. Invented spelling is a temporary method that a writer uses to get ideas down on paper. It should not be equated with proper spelling.

Irregular. An exception to the normal linguistic pattern or rule. Spellings such as *done, laugh, through, enough,* are irregular spellings. *Good, better, best* are exceptions to the *-er, -est* pattern for the comparative and superlative of adjectives and therefore irregular.

Linguistics. The scientific study of language. Linguistics includes phonology (sounds), morphology (internal structure of words), syntax (manner in which words combine), and semantics (meaning).

Monosyllable. A word made up of only one sound or syllable: *do, come, straight.*

Morpheme. The smallest meaningful unit in the language. A morpheme can consist of a word or a part of a word. The words *man, wait,* and *noun,* for example, are morphemes. Prefixes like *re-, un-,* and *pre-* and suffixes like *-ly, -ness,* and *-en* are morphemes because they are meaningful parts of a word.

Noun. The name of a person, place, thing, or idea. Nouns can be classified as common nouns, or the general category of persons, places, and things (*dog, child, teacher*). Nouns can also be classified as proper nouns (*Helen, Chicago, Ford Motors*), abstract nouns (*goodness, honesty, bravery*), singular nouns (*car, desk, book*), or plural nouns (*cars, desks, books*).

Onset and rime. Parts of spoken language that are smaller than syllables but larger than phonemes. The onset is the initial consonant(s) sound of a syllable (*b-* as in *bag*). The rime is the part of the syllable that contains the vowel and all that follows (*-ag* as in *bag*).

Orthography. A part of linguistics that deals with understanding the sounds of the language and their representation in alphabetical symbols. Orthography is concerned primarily with the spelling of English.

Phoneme. The speech sound of English produced by a grapheme, or letter: the *m* in *mat,* the *j* in *joy.* Some phonemes are represented by a combination of letters: /th/, /sh/, /ee/, /oa/, /ei/. Some letters may represent more than one phoneme: *c* as in *cat* and *cite; y* as in *yes, by,* and *nicely; o* as in *come* and *home.*

Phonemic awareness. The awareness that written words can be thought of as a sequence of phonemes and using those sounds to make and identify words. Phonemic awareness is a subcategory of phonological awareness.

Phonemics. A part of phonological linguistics that studies and analyzes phonemes or sounds of the language.

Phonetics. A branch of physiology that studies the production, transmission, and reception of speech sounds.

Phonics. A method of teaching reading, spelling, and pronunciation that emphasizes learning the sounds of letters and combinations of letters in order to figure out, or sound out, unfamiliar words.

Phonogram. A sequence of letters consisting of a vowel grapheme and a consonant grapheme at the end of a word that represents a common ending sound and can produce many words by adding an initial consonant sound: *-ing* as used in *sing, bring, ring, king,* etc.

Phonological awareness. A broad term that includes phonemic awareness. In addition to phonemes, phonological awareness activities can include rhymes, words, syllables, and onset and rimes.

Phonology. The systematic study of the sound system of a language and how it functions. The goal of phonology is to understand and internalize sounds of the language in order to communicate.

Plural. A word that represents more than one: *children, books, candies.*

Polysyllabic word. A word made up of two or more syllables.

Prefix. An affix or morpheme added to the beginning of a word to change the word's meaning or make a new word: *man–superman, happy–unhappy, new–renew.*

Print awareness. Awareness of how print (printed material) works and how it looks. It includes such concepts as the following: print is made up of letters, letters make up words, words make up sentences, sentences are read from left to right.

R-controlled sound. The modified vowel sound that comes about when the vowel is followed by *r* in the same syllable: *care, never, fire, cure.*

Reading. The process of getting meaning from printed language. Reading involves recognition of words and understanding of the meaning of words. Reading is communication of the writer to the reader.

Root word. A word without a prefix or suffix. A word before a prefix or suffix has been added.

Semantics. The study or science of the relationship of signs and symbols to what they represent to their interpreters. Understanding the meaning of words.

Sight words. Words recognized by sight rather than being sounded out phonetically. Words with irregular or unusual spelling patterns are called sight words to denote how they ought to be taught: *said, laugh, enough.*

Silent letters. Letters in a word that are not pronounced, but that also must not be omitted when spelling or writing the word: *lamb, knew, often.*

Singular. A word that represents only one.

Spelling. Naming or writing the letters of a word in proper order; the process of encoding, or putting, spoken sounds and words into written symbols.

Suffix. An affix or morpheme added to the end of a word to alter or change its meaning: *kind–kindness, dark–darker, force–forcefully.*

Syllable. A unit of spoken language consisting of a single uninterrupted sound formed by a vowel or diphthong alone or with a consonant. A syllable always contains a vowel sound, or it may have a vowel-consonant combination such as **V** (vowel only), **CV** (consonant/vowel), **VC** (vowel/consonant), **CVC** (consonant/vowel/consonant). The word go has one syllable. The word understanding has four syllables.

Syllabication.   The division of a word into syllables.

Synonym.   A word that has the same or nearly the same meaning as another word in the same language: *beautiful–gorgeous, evil–bad, funny–humorous.*

Syntax.   The manner in which words are combined to form phrases and sentences. Rules that govern the use of the language.

Verb.   A word that expresses action or state of being. Every complete sentence must contain a verb.

Vowel phoneme.   One of two groups of sounds (the other being consonant phonemes). Vowels are reproduced by vibration of the vocal cords with no stoppage of the outgoing air. English contains five vowels (*a, e, i, o, u*) and one sometimes-vowel (*y*), which, by themselves or in combination with other vowels, produce approximately twenty-two vowel phonemes or sounds.

FEDERAL EDUCATION LAW GLOSSARY

Academic Standards.   Guidelines for what every student should know and achieve in a variety of subjects, such as reading, math, science, etc.

Accountability system.   Each state sets standards for what each child is expected to know. Student achievement is measured for every child every year. The results of these tests are reported to the public.

Achievement gap.   The difference between how low-income and minority children learn as compared with the majority of children their age.

Assessment.   Educational evaluations in the form of grades, or tests, whereby a student's achievement or progress is compared to a norm, or average, of all students' performance.

AYP (Adequate Yearly Progress).   The minimum level of achievement that a state or school district must meet each year toward 100 percent achievement by the year 2014 (NCLB guidelines).

ESEA (Elementary and Secondary Education Act).   The primary federal law affecting federal funding of education in the U.S. It was enacted into law in 1965. The latest revision signed by President Bush in 2002 is known as the No Child Left Behind Act.

LEA (Local Education Agency).   The public board of education that oversees public schools within a city, township, district, or other political subdivisions.

NCLB (No Child Left Behind).   A revision of the Elementary and Secondary Education Act passed by Congress in 2001 and signed by President Bush in 2002 that increases testing, reporting, and other government requirements on all public schools.

NEAP (National Assessment of Educational Progress). National tests of what American students know and can do in various subject areas.

SEA (State Education Agency). The public board of education or other governing body that oversees state administration of public education programs.

Title I. The first section of the ESEA. Title I provides additional federal spending for America's most disadvantaged school districts. It is used to improve the teaching and learning of children in high-poverty schools to meet the challenges of state academic content and performance standards.

References

Adams, M. J. (1998). *Beginning to read: Thinking and learning about print* (2nd ed.). Cambridge: MIT Press.

Alexander, D. (2005, September 28). National Institutes of Health News Alert. Washington, DC: U.S. Government Printing Office.

Ambruster, B. B., Lehr, F., & Osborn, J. (2005). *Putting children first.* Ann Arbor, MI: Center for the Improvement of Early Reading Achievement.

Anderson, R. C., Hilbert, E. H., Scott, J. A., & Wilkenson, I. A. G. (1985). *Becoming a nation of readers: The report of the commission of reading.* Urbana, IL: Center for the Study of Reading.

Anderson, S. (2003). *The book of reading and writing ideas, tips, and lists for the elementary classroom.* Thousand Oaks, CA: Corwin Press.

Artley, A. S. (1996, September). Controversial issues relating to word perception. *The Reading Teacher, 50*(1), 10–13.

Aukerman, R. C. (1984). *Approaches to beginning reading.* New York: Wiley.

Baumann, J. E., Hoffman, J. V., Moon, J., & Duffy-Hester, A. M. (1998). Where are the teachers' voices in the phonics/whole language debate? (Results from a survey of U.S. elementary classroom teachers). *The Reading Teacher, 51*(8), 636–650.

Bear, M. J., Invernizzi, M., & Templeton, S. (2004). *Words their way: Word study for phonics, vocabulary, and spelling instruction* (3rd ed.). New York: Macmillan Merrill.

Bell, T. (1983). *A nation at risk.* Washington, DC: U.S. Department of Education, National Commission of Excellence in Education.

Berger, P. (1998). Portfolio folly. *Education Week, 17*(18), 76.

Blevins, W. (1998). *Phonics from A to Z.* New York: Scholastic Books.

Block, C., & Israel S. (2005). *Reading first and beyond.* Thousand Oaks, CA: Corwin Press.

Bond, G. L., & Dykstra, R. (1967). The cooperative research program in first grade reading instruction. *Reading Research Quarterly, 2,* 5–142.

Bonnema, H. (1961). Writing by sound: A new method of teaching reading. *Spelling Progress Bulletin, 6,* 1.

Bowen, J. A., & Francis, J. (1991). Phonological analysis as a function of age and exposure to reading instruction. *Applied Psycholinguistics, 12,* 91–121.

Burgess, A. (1975). *Language made plain* (rev. ed.) London: Fontana.

Burns, B. (2006). *How to teach balanced reading and writing,* (2nd ed.). Thousand Oaks, CA: Corwin Press.

California Department of Education. (1995). *Every child a reader: The report of the California reading task force.* Sacramento, CA: Author.

California Department of Education. (1996). *California initiative in reading. Teaching reading: A balanced comprehensive approach to teaching reading in prekindergarten through grade three.* Sacramento, CA: Author.

California Department of Education. (1996). *Teaching reading: A balanced, comprehensive approach to teaching reading in prekindergarten through grade three.* Sacramento, CA: Author.

California Department of Education. (1997). *English-language arts content standards for California public schools, K–12.* Sacramento, CA: Author.

Cambell, J. R., Donahue, P. M., Reese, C. M., & Philips, G. W. (1996). *Reading report card for the nation and the states: Findings from the national assessment of educational progress (NAEP) and trial assessment (1994).* Washington, DC: U.S. Department of Education.

Carrol, J. B., Davies, P., & Richman, P. (1971). *American Heritage word frequency book.* Boston: Houghton Mifflin.

Chall, J. S. (1967). *Learning to read: The great debate.* New York: Harcourt.

Clymer, T. (1963). The utility of generalizations in the primary grades. *The Reading Teacher, 16*(6), 183–187.

Collins, J. (1997, October 27). How Johnny should read. *Time, 150*(17), 78–81.

Cunningham, P. (2005). *Phonics they use: words for reading and writing* (4th ed.). Boston: Pearson/Allyn & Bacon.

Daniels, J. C., & Diack, H. (1956). *Progress in reading.* Nottingham: University of Nottingham Institute of Education.

Downing, J. A. (1965). *The initial teaching alphabet.* New York: Macmillan.

Dr. Maggie's classroom phonics readers. (2006). San Diego, CA: Teaching Resource Center.

Ehri, L. C. (1995). Phrases of development in learning to read words by sight. *Journal of Research in Reading, 18*(2), 116–125.

Feitelson, D., & Golstein, Z. (1986). Patterns of book ownership and reading to young children. *Reading Teacher, 39*(9), 924–930.

Flesch, R. (1955). *Why Johnny can't read.* New York: Harper & Row.

Flesch, R. (1981). *Why Johnny still can't read.* New York: Harper & Row.

Florida Department of Education. (1991). *Sunshine state standards overview.* Tallahassee, FL: Author.

Freppon, P. A., & Dahl, K. L. (1998). Balanced reading instruction: Insights and considerations. *Reading Research Quarterly, 33*(2), 240–251.

Fry, E. (1995). *How to teach reading.* Laguna Beach, CA: Laguna Beach Educational Books.

Fry, E. (2004). *How to teach reading* (4th ed.). Westminster, CA: Teacher Created Materials.

Fry, E., Kress, J., & Fountoukidis, D. L. (2005). *The reading teacher's book of lists* (4th ed.). San Francisco: Jossey-Bass.

Furness, E. L. (1990). *Guide to better English spelling.* Lincolnwood, IL: National Textbook Co.

Gagen, M. (2005). *Phonemic awareness.* National Right to Read Foundation, Manassas Park, VA. Retrieved May 2005 from www.righttrackreading.com

Gaskins, I. W., Ehri, L. C., Cress, C., O'Hara, C., & Donnelly, K. (1996). Making discoveries about words. *The Reading Teacher, 50*(4), 312–327.

Gattegno, C. (1962). *Words in color.* Chicago: Learning Materials.

Gray, L. (1963). *Teaching children to read.* New York: Ronald Press.

Gray, W. S., & Arbuthnot, M. (1946). *Our new friends* (Books 1–2). Chicago: Scott Foresman.

Griffith, P. L., & Olson, M. W. (1992). Phonemic awareness helps beginning readers break the code. *The Reading Teacher, 45*(7), 516–525.

Hanna, P. A., Hanna, J. L., Hodge, R. E., & Rudolph, E. H. (1966). *Phoneme-grapheme correspondence as clues to spelling improvement.* Washington, DC: U.S. Department of Education.

Hawaii Department of Education. (2005). *Accountability.* Retrieved from http://reach.k12.hi.us/accountability/

Heilman, A. W. (1966). *Phonics in proper perspective.* Columbus, OH: Merrill.

Heilman, A. W. (2002). *Phonics in proper perspective* (9th ed.). Upper Saddle River, NJ: Merrill.

Heilman, A. W., Blair, T. R., & Rupley, W. H. (2001). *Principles and practices of teaching reading* (10th ed.). Upper Saddle River, NJ: Prentice Hall.

Hempenstall, K. (1997). *The role of phonics in learning to read: What does research say?* Melbourne, Australia: Royal Melbourne Institute of Technology.

Hempenstall, K. (2003). *Phonemic awareness: What does it mean?* A 2003 update. Retrieved on September 28, 2005, from www.educationnews.org

Hempenstall, K. (2005). Some issues in phonics instruction: Implicit and explicit phonics instruction. Retrieved on October 10, 2005, from www.education news.org

Honig, B. (2000). *Teaching our children to read: The role of skills in a comprehensive reading program* (2nd ed.). Thousand Oaks, CA: Corwin Press.

Institute of Educational Services. (1996). Data from National Assessment of Educational Progress. Washington, DC: U.S. Department of Education.

International Reading Association. (1998). *Phonemic awareness and the teaching of Reading: A position statement.* Newark, DE: Author.

International Reading Association. (1998). *The role of phonics in reading instruction: A position statement.* Newark, DE: Author.

International Reading Association, & National Association for the Education of Young Children. (1998). *Learning to read and write: Developmentally appropriate practices for young children: A joint position statement.* Newark, DE: Author.

Jesness, J. (2005). *Teaching English language learners K–12.* Thousand Oaks, CA: Corwin Press.

Jones, R. (1996, June). Skimishes on the reading front. *American School Board Journal, 183*(6), 15–18.

Kendall, J. S., & Marzano, R. (1997). *Content knowledge: A compendium of standards and benchmarks for K–12 education* (2nd ed.). Aurora, CO: Mid-Continent Regional Educational Laboratory.

Laframboise, K. (1996, January–February). Developmental spelling in the fourth grade: an analysis of what poor readers do. *Reading Horizons, 36,* 231–248.

Larsen, J., & Eastin, D. (1997). *A message from the state superintendent of public instruction: English-language arts content standards for California public schools.* Sacramento: California Board of Education.

Mauer, D. M., & Kamhi, A. G. (1996). Factors that influence phoneme-grapheme correspondence learning. *Journal of Learning Disabilities, 29,* 259–70.

Mayzner, M. S., & Tresselt, M. E. (1965). Tables of single-letter and digram frequency counts for various word-length and letter-position combinations. *Psychonomics Monograph Supplements,* 13–32.

Mazurkiewicz, A., & Tanyzer, H. (1966). *Easy-to-read i/t/a/ program.* New York: Initial Teaching Alphabet Publications.

McCulloch, M. (1996). *Phonics is phonics is phonics—or is it?* Beaverton, OR: Riggs Institute Internet Publication. Retrieved from www.riggsinst.org

McGuiness, D. (1997). *Why our children can't read.* New York: Free Press.

Michigan Department of Education. (1995). *Michigan language arts: Model content standards for curriculum and benchmarks.* Lansing, MI: Author.

National Center for Educational Statistics. (2003). *Nation's report card.* Washington, DC: U.S. Department of Education.

National Commission on Excellence in Education. (1983). *A nation at risk.* Washington, DC: U.S. Department of Education.

National Institute for Literacy (NIFL). (2005). *Putting reading first.* Retrieved on November 1, 2005, from www.nifl.gov/nifl/publications.html

National Institute of Child Health Development. (2005). *Report on the National Reading Panel and combinations of teaching phonics.* Washington, DC: U.S. Government Printing Office.

National Reading Panel. (2000, updated 2005, September 28, & 2005, October 26). *Teaching children to read.* Washington, DC: U.S. Government Printing Office.

National Reading Panel. (2000). *Teaching children to read: Reports of the subgroups.* Washington DC: U.S. Government Printing Office.

National Reading Panel. (2005). *Frequently asked questions.* Washington, DC: U.S. Government Printing Office.

Neuman, R., & Celano, D. (2001). Access to print in low income and middle income communities: An ecological study of four neighborhoods. *Reading Research Quarterly, 36*(1), 8–26.

Pei, M. (1967). *The story of the English language.* New York: Simon & Schuster.

Peregoy, S. F., & Boyle, O. F. (1997). *Reading, writing, and learning in ESL: A resource book for K–12 teachers* (2nd ed.). White Plains, NY: Longman.

Pitman J., & St. John, J. (1969). *Alphabets and reading.* London: Pitman.

READ XL. (2006). New York: Scholastic Press. *Rhymes without reason.* Lake Placid, NY: Spelling Reform Association.

Riley, R. (1998). *Riley issues five challenges: The first national reading summit news release.* Washington, DC: U.S. Department of Education.

Smith, E. B., Goodman, K., & Meredith, R. (1970). *Language and thinking in the elementary school.* New York: Holt, Rinehart & Winston.

Smith, F. (2004). *Understanding reading* (6th ed.). Mahwah, NJ: Erlbaum Associates.

Smith, N. B. (1986). *American reading instruction.* Newark, DE: International Reading Association.

Smith, N. B. (2002). *American reading instruction* (special ed.). Newark, DE: International Reading Association.

Snow, C. E., Burns, M. S., & Griffin, P. (1998). *Preventing reading difficulties in young children.* Washington, DC: National Academy Press.

Stahl, S. A. (1992). Saying the "p" word: Nine guidelines for exemplary phonics instruction. *The Reading Teacher, 45*(8), 618–625.

Stahl, S. A., Duffy-Hester, A. M., & Dougherty-Stahl, K. A. (1998, July–September). Everything you always wanted to know about phonics (but were afraid to ask). *Reading Research Quarterly, 33*(3), 338–355.

Standford, J. (1997). *Message from the superintendent.* Seattle, WA: Seattle Public Schools.

Starrett, E. V. (1970). *My phonics manual.* Birmingham, MI: Midwest Publications.

Starrett, E. V. (1981). *Spelling reform proposals for the English language.* Dissertation, Wayne State University, University Microfilms International.

Strickland, D. (1995). Reinventing our literacy programs: Books, basics, balance. *The Reading Teacher, 48*(4), 294–302.

Strickland, D. (1998). *Teaching phonics today: A primer for educators.* Newark, DE: International Reading Association.

Study shows that half of the adults in U.S. can't read or handle arithmetic. (1993, September 9). *New York Times,* p. 1.

Texas Department of Education. (1998). *Texas essential knowledge and skills for English language and reading.* Austin, TX: Author.

U.S. Department of Education. (1996). *National assessment of educational progress.* Washington, DC: U.S. Government Printing Office.

U.S. Department of Education. (2003). *A parent's guide to No Child Left Behind.* Washington, DC: U.S. Government Printing Office.

U.S. Department of Education. (2004). *Early Reading First and Reading First.* Washington, DC: U.S. Government Printing Office. Retrieved from www.ed.gov/programs

U.S. Department of Education. (2005). *Teacher to teacher initiative.* Washington, DC: U.S. Government Printing Office.

U.S. Department of Education. (2006, April). *No child left behind is working.* Retrieved from www.ed.gov/nclb

U.S. Department of Education. (n.d.). *No child left behind: A toolkit for teachers.* Retrieved May 10, 2006, from www.ed.gov/nclb/overview

U.S. Department of Education, Office of Educational Research and Improvement. (1993). *Adult literacy in America.* Washington, DC: U.S. Government Printing Office.

Wagstaff, J. M. (1997). Building practical knowledge of letter-sound correspondences: A beginner's word wall and beyond. *The Reading Teacher, 51*(4), 298–304.

Webster, N. (1789). *Dissertations on the English language.* Boston: Isaiah Thomas Co.

Webster's New World Dictionary. (1998). New York: Wiley.

White, T. G., Swell, J., & Yanagehara, A. (1989, January). Teaching elementary students to use word-part clues. *The Reading Teacher, 42*(4), 302–308.

Wilson, R. M., & Hall, M. A. (1997). *Programmed word attack for teachers.* Columbus, OH: Merrill.

Wylie, R. E., & Durrell, D. D. (1970). Teaching vowels through phonograms. *Elementary English, 47,* 787–791.

Yopp, H. K. (1992). Developing phonemic awareness in young children. *The Reading Teacher, 45*(9), 696–703.

Yopp, H. K. (1995). Read-aloud books for developing phonemic awareness: An animated bibliography. *The Reading Teacher, 48*(6), 538–543.

Index

CORWIN PRESS